VASILY SES

EXPERIENCE, FOF
THE QUESTION ᴏꜰ ʙᴇɪɴɢ

On the Boundary of Two Worlds: Identity, Freedom, and Moral Imagination in the Baltics

7

VASILY SESEMANN
EXPERIENCE, FORMALISM, AND THE QUESTION OF BEING

Thorsten Botz-Bornstein

Preface by Eero Tarasti

Amsterdam - New York, NY 2006

©Cover photo: "Vyborg", by Eeli Aalto

The paper on which this book is printed meets the requirements of "ISO 9706:1994, Information and documentation - Paper for documents - Requirements for permanence".

ISBN-10: 90-420-2092-X
ISBN-13: 978-90-420-2092-4
©Editions Rodopi B.V., Amsterdam - New York, NY 2006
Printed in the Netherlands

Contents

Wilhelm Sesemann in the Context of Semiotics

Eero Tarasti

We now know that Wilhelm Sesemann was the greatest philosopher in the history of Lithuania. Thorsten Botz-Bornstein's study is the first "western" treatise to take him seriously in that regard, and to explore carefully the relationships between Sesemann's thought and the Russian and German philosophy of his time. As Botz-Bornstein observes, however, Sesemann's thought comes at us from so many angles, it is difficult to define the "real" philosophy of this Baltic thinker.

In Finland, interest in Sesemann's work has stemmed mostly from its connection to semiotics. His name first surfaced here around 1982, when semiotics began to gain a foothold in our country, and the Semiotic Society of Finland began its annual meetings. The third of those, held in Jyväskylä in 1983, represented a notable expansion of Finnish semiotics onto the international scene. Among the featured speakers was Henri Broms (1985) and the great Franco-Lithuanian scholar, Algirdas Julien Greimas, who had lectured in Helsinki as early as 1979. Also featured was the Finnish psychiatrist and writer Oscar Parland (1912–1997), who later became an honorary member of our society. He and his brother, the Finnish-Swedish poet Henry Parland (1908–1930), were nephews of Wilhelm Sesemann. When Henry was declared the "First Finnish semiotician," interest began to grow in how and where he had gotten his ideas on semiotics. Oscar Parland, in lectures at meetings of the Finnish Semiotic Society, spoke about the Parland-Sesemann family history, and how Henry got his ideas about Russian formalism from his uncle, Sesemann. In those lectures, Oscar told breathtaking stories about Sesemann, his exile to Siberia, and his subsequent rehabilitation. The lectures were first published in *Synteesi* in 1991 and included in a collection entitled *Tieto ja eläytyminen: Esseitä ja muistelmia* (*Knowledge and Empathy: Essays and Reminiscences*).

At about the same time, Greimas, my former teacher in Paris, began to promote Lithuanian patrimony. He spoke of Sesemann having taught at Kaunas University when he was a student there, and told me about a study that Sesemann had written on aesthetics, which I determined to have translated into English. In our correspondence on the matter, Greimas mentioned a son of Sesemann living in Paris as an immigrant, but doubted that he would have been a pupil of his father. Hence any opinions about "Finnish" roots of Sesemann's thought are speculative, and based on the internal content of his doctrine.

Of course, an essential moment in the development of European semiotics was that of Russian Formalism, and the Preface to Sesemann's *Estetika* was written by the formalist Zirmunsky, well-known for his studies in metrics. (My knowledge of that preface is limited to Zirmunsky's mention of Yury Tynianov, among the names of other Russian formalists.) Oscar Parland considered it obvious that Henry's ideas about Russian Formalism came from their uncle, Sesemann, who had gotten them from Zirmunsky.

In 1990, I commented on Sesemann in an article written (in both Finnish and English) for the Nordic art review, *Siksi*, from which I dare to quote:

> It would be tempting to draw connections between the neo-Kantian philosophy and epistemology of Sesemann and Greimas's semiotics, but at least in practice there was no interaction between the two men. The fact that Greimas returned to the subject/object problem in his "third semiotic revolution" was due to quite different reasons than Sesemann's philosophy. Nevertheless, some thoughts Sesemann had were quite close to those of Greimas. One of these was the differentiation between the concepts *Wissen* and *Kennen*. Since then, the French philosopher Vladimir Jankélévitch has spoken in the same manner about the difference between *savoir* and *connaissance*: the former denotes knowledge acquired from books; the latter, knowledge based on personal acquaintance. Perhaps Greimas' modality of 'know' (*savoir*), should also be divided into those two types, according to his own categories of exteroceptive/interoceptive.... (Tarasti 1990: 17).

Only a year after my article appeared, Oscar Parland's *Empathy and Knowledge* (1991) was published, which contained a more detailed explication of Sesemann's philosophy. In Parland's view, the essential dichotomy – and common thread – in Sesemann's thought is the distinction between objective and subjective knowledge (*Gegenständliche und ungegenständliche Erkenntnis*).

Fundamental to objective knowledge is the separation between subject (perceiver) and object (perceived). To gain such knowledge thus requires a kind of reduction that attempts to bracket all subjective elements from the act of perception or sensation (*Erkenntnis*). In the act of conceptualization, the subject tries to dominate, take over, and assimilate the object, which appears as a transcendental entity to a subject that is alien to it. The subject grasps the object and detaches it from the *Umwelt* in which it has been embedded. Extracted from its "native" habitat, the object is set before the subject, to be observed, in terms of Kantian categories, as a "thing" (*Gegenstand*). Most important to the described process is the external appearance (*Erscheinung*) of the object, that is to say, the medium or phenomenon by which it appears to a subject.

That process often involves violence – what Sesemann calls *vergewaltigen* – to the object, particularly when such observation is directed to living entities or to psychic, spiritual, and similar phenomena. Objective knowledge alone (*Erkennen*) becomes less and less satisfactory, the deeper we proceed into the realm of psychic realities; the intellectual violence grows, causing distortions of knowledge to multiply:

Subject _____ Object

We can see in the above discussion a critique of Husserl – oft-mentioned in Sesemann studies – and an anticipation of Heidegger's principle of *Gelassenheit* (letting things be), or in the semiotic terms of Charles Morris, "lettings things happen."

At the opposite pole lies non-objective (*ungegenständliche*) knowledge, or *Wissen*, such as that of realities connected with morals, religion, or aesthetic phenomena. This kind of knowledge differs most radically from the objective kind, in that it makes no clear distinction between subject and object. The subject is part of the reality that it experiences; and that experience necessarily includes the subject's self-knowledge as well as the subject's consciousness of itself (*Erlebnis*, personal experience). The subject recognizes itself in the object, and temporarily shifts to the latter's side, yet without separating the object from its proper *Umwelt*. In this act the subject is "split" into two halves: one part of the subject remains as subject; the other part shifts to the object, with which it fuses:

subject _____ subject + object
_____

Sesemann's notion of *Wissen* has its counterpart in the so-called "Third semiotic revolution" sparked by Greimas, who after his hyper-objective, "linguistics phase" (e.g., Greimas 1966), began to figure subjective aspects into his semiotic theories, via the concept of *modalities* (e.g., Greimas 1973). He implicitly acknowledged as much in a speech given at the *Kalevala* symposium in Paris in 1985, when he said the ancient Finns were not so stupid as to have worshiped mere objects, stones, trees, and so on, but rather, the *spirit* in those objects. He moreover claimed to have more empathy with German-romantic ethnology than with that of positivists, which only gather things and classify them – an attitude also taken by Sesemann.

In what follows, my assessment of Sesemann's thought is based on copies of several of his studies, which were kindly sent to me by Greimas and Oscar Parland: *Beiträge zum Erkenntnisproblem III: Das Logisch-Rationale* (1930); *Die logischen Gesetze im Verhältnis zum subjektbezogenen und psychischen Sein* (1931); *Estetika and Musu laiku gnoseologijai naujai besiorientuojant* (1935a); and *Zum Problem der logischen Paradoxien* (1935b). Those texts can be re-read in many ways, and Botz-Bornstein's reading of them in the light of Lacan and Bakhtin seems completely justifiable: Oscar Parland tells us that Sesemann knew Freud and admired his treatise on dreams; and as mentioned above, Sesemann's contact with Russian Formalism was real, given his personal friendship with Zirmunsky.

We can also read Sesemann in the framework of "existential semiotics," which I have been developing for some time now (e.g., Tarasti 2000). In my theories, the "classic" semiotic doctrines remain valid, especially that of Greimas, but influences also flow into it from German philosophy (Hegel, Kant, Jaspers, Heidegger) as well as from Kierkegaard, Sartre, de Beauvoir, Jean Wahl and others. That variety of sources mirrors the influences on Sesemann's thought, and hence provides a suitable framework for my interpretation of his writings in terms of Greimassian and/or existential semiotics, to which Sesemann is shown to be a precursor.

First of all, almost anywhere he uses the term "logical" we can replace it with the term "semiotical." Sesemann always underlines the fact that he is studying the logical structure of the world and not its psychological content, as is the case with Greimassian as well as existential semiotics. Further, as a musicologist, I find interesting his analysis of *der Schall*, or "sound" (Sesemann 1931: 114). He, like Ernst Kurth, urges us to identify music not with printed notes but with *Schall*, which is equally translatable as "noise" (a radical anticipation of Futurism!). Once a sound has been emitted from its object, it creates its own universe:

> Daher vermag auch das Geräusch und insbesondere der Ton, als ein von aller Dinglichkeit losgelöstes Phänomen eine selbständige Existenz zu führen: worauf die Möglichkeit beruht in Gestalt der Musik eine eigenständige autonome Tonwelt zu schaffen (ibid.).

Therefore sound, and especially the tone, as a phenomenon freed from all materiality, may lead an independent existence: on which basis rests the potentiality, in the form of music, for shaping an independent, autonomous tone-world.

It is interesting that the chapter entitled *Die logischen Gesetze und das daseinsautonome Sein* starts with a question about the nature of 'becoming': "Is that modality established on logical principles? [Ist das Werden den logischen Prinzipien unterworfen?]" (121). That question brings to mind the time Greimas asked me to write an article for his *Dictionnaire* on the modality of 'becoming' (*devenir, Werden*), which was inserted into the otherwise rather static, atemporal categories of his system. Sesemann has this to say about 'becoming' (122): "Das Werden als Einheit von Sein und Nichtsein ist also das einzig, das wahrhaft Reale" [Becoming, as a unity of Being and Not-Being, is thus the only, the genuinely real]."

Sesemann discusses the problem of reducing 'becoming' to points of rest (*Ruhemomenten*), an issue one also encounters in using the Greimassian semiotic square, which is based on contrary relations between S1 and S2 and their negations, non-S1 and non-S2. Here Zeno's paradox comes into play: we can try to temporalize the square by following the movement within it, among its various categories; but at the same time, the static, fixed points of reference remain in place. In that way, movement is conceived as spatialized: "Umdeutung der Dynamik der Bewegung in statisch räumliches Sein" [a new meaning of the dynamics of motion in static, spatial being]" (130).

Pertinent in this context is the Bergsonian distinction, also mentioned by Sesemann, between "physical" and "phenomenal" (concrete) time. Sesemann notes that spatialization also means objectification (*Vergegenständlichung*), which is not the same as conceptualization. According to Sesemann, we can study time only when we step into it: "... als man in ihr drinsteht oder vielmehr mit ihr geht, also soweit als man selbst zeitlich ist und diese Zeitlichkeit unmittlebar anschaut" [... to the extent that one steps into [time] – or, even further, goes with it – that is, to the extent to which one is temporal, and to which one perceives that temporality directly]" (ibid.).

Sesemann's reflections on the essence of logical negation are precursors of ideas that Greimas incorporated into his semiotic square. The contradictory opposition must be specified as a contrary relation: "Wir haben nicht mehr a und non-a sondern a und b vor uns" [We no longer confront a and non-a, but both a and b]" (138). Sesemann deems such motion an aporia, i.e., an unresolvable paradox.

Sesemann links the dialectics of 'becoming' to the notion of the possible: "... das Bestimmtwerden als Unbestimmtheit an einer Bestimmtheit oder als Bestimmtheit eines Unbestimmt-seins" [...determinate becoming as indeterminate becoming or as the determination of an indeterminate [state of] being]." We find parallels to that view in existential semiotics, where we speak of three modes of signs: (1) *presigns* – inchoate signs, those which are only starting to become signs, and as such are not yet fixed; (2) *act-signs*, which are clearly determinable (*bestimmt*); (3) and *post-signs*. Presigns are located in the realm of possibility, and are therefore virtual (Tarasti 2000: 33). Sesemann likewise says that the concept of the possible is the foundation for the conceptual presentation of 'becoming'. In a chapter on *Werden und Identität*, Sesemann asks if 'becoming' has identity, and concludes that it does. In doing so, he comes close to the Hegelian notion of *an-sich-sein* and *für-sich-sein* – or in my reformulation, *an-mich-sein* and *für-mich-sein,* the latter of which refers precisely to the identity of a subject.

Sesemann then ponders the category of *ideal-Allgemeine* (the ideally general), which equates to the notion of "transcendence" in existential semiotics. Sesemann criticizes the dominant school of thought, which commits to a conceptual realism that leads to objectification (*Vergegenständlichung*) of the general, and mistakenly takes the latter as an original phenomenon. To Sesemann, that is the pitfall of Husserl's method (173).

When first reading that passage in Sesemann, some twenty years ago, I noticed even then his distinction between the real and the possible (*Wirklich/Möglich*). The real, as real, is always something concrete and actual – an act-sign, in the parlance of existential semiotics – because it is real only insofar it is active (*wirksam*). Therefore, it follows that the relation of the possible to the real is something concretely actual. The possible itself, in its primal given-ness, is concretely actual. It signifies the plenitude (*Fülle*) of possibilities which are concealed in a real, actual situation. Regarding this issue, Sesemann formulates a highly interesting axiom (175): "... das Allgemeine als Fülle der konkreten Möglichkeit ist ein konstitutives (wesentliches) Moment der Zeitlichkeit selbst in ihrem aktuellen Sein" [... the general, as a plenitude of concrete possibilities, is a constitutive [essential] moment of temporality itself in its actual being]." To my mind, Sesemann's comments bring up the notions of immanent and manifest, as they appear particularly in musical composition; for example, in the construction of a theme (possible, immanent) and the actual appearance of it (real, manifest). In existential semiotics, the same notions help describe how the transcendental becomes actual in *Dasein*, how the *pleroma* (fullness, plenitude) of the second act of transcendence might be interpreted more precisely as a *plenitude of possibilities.*

When Sesemann ponders the relation between formal and transcendental logics, he provides semioticians with clues as to how signs, in transcendence, function as pre-signs of *Dasein.* Sesemann himself uses the term "pre-logical" (1930: 145), and describes the logical sphere as timeless. (In our theory, that would mean a transcendence that is antinarrative and achronic.) He goes on to underlines the act-like, processual nature of the logical, and here again, the term "logical" can be translated profitably into "semiotical."

I suppose this might be enough evidence of how Sesemann can be brought directly into past and present debates about semiotics and its epistemological foundations. Thorsten Botz-Bornstein's profound and rich inquiry opens up paths leading to the core of Sesemann's philosophy. Sesemann's voice is again heard in the history of European and Lithuanian philosophy, as well as on the contemporary scene of thought and actuality.

Experience as a Subject of Philosophy in the Early Twentieth Century

This book deals with the thoughts of the philosopher Vasily Sesemann whose originality becomes clear in the following chapters. In these chapters, some philosophical topics that are central in Sesemann's philosophy are introduced, explained, and put into the philosophical context of their time. In the present introduction, I will to single out what I believe to be among the most important of these thoughts, draw attention to its exceptional status within Western philosophy, and also point to its relationship with certain Eastern models of thinking.

This thought is Sesemann's idea of *experience as a component of life that cannot and should not be objectified*. Sesemann develops this idea by reflecting it against various topics: empathy, *Erkenntnistheorie* (theory of knowledge), Formalism, Freudian psychoanalysis, Bergson's philosophy of time... At two points in this book,

Sesemann's idea of experience will be examined in detail. In Chapter 2, I show that Sesemann's idea of "experience" is reminiscent of that of Dilthey, the author of "Psychologie als Erfahrungswissenschaft." In Chapter 3, I explain the reasons for Sesemann's opposition to any reduction of psychic life to abstract psychic elements. However, since Sesemann also discusses experience – though more indirectly – in connection with several other subjects, I suggest seeing "experience" as a guideline leading through his roughly fifty years of philosophizing.

Sesemann in 1912

For Sesemann, experience is dynamic, constantly self-reflective and therefore "ungraspable" in both an objective and a subjective way. In 1927 he wrote: "The knowledge of my experience is not added, so to speak, from the outside, as an Other or something new to what has been experienced. It is an immediate growth out of its original consciousness or self-consciousness."[1]

Psychology fails to grasp this experience because it tends to describe multi-layered psychic phenomena like will, judgment, or evaluation, as

Not to box experience
up but to experience-experience.

"appearances" rendered in the form of "sentiments" or "imaginations."
Sesemann urges us to recognize that these appearances are only shadows of
"real" psychic life or "real" psychic experience.

Sesemann puts forward his ideas about experience so nonchalantly
that readers run the risk of not recognizing the unique position these remarks occupy in the history of philosophy. Where else has experience and
the problem of grasping it with the help of philosophical or scientific approaches been described in such a way? Or, perhaps first, where else has
experience been described at all?

Etymology
of experience

The word "experience" itself has a double sense already contained
in its Latin root. *Experiri* means both "to feel," in the sense of the German
Erleben, and "to try" or "to attempt" in the sense of making (scientific)
experiments. The Russian word "опыт" expresses even more directly the
double meaning of "personal experience" *and* (scientific) experiment. The
Greek *empeiria* which signifies "to attempt," "to endeavor," or "to experiment," gave, in accordance with the latter part of the Latin meaning, its
name to that branch of philosophy which prefers to see "experience" as
something objectified and measurable. The forefathers of empiricism, the
British philosophers of the sixteenth and seventeenth centuries, Locke,
Berkeley, and Hume, established experience solely in this way, neglecting
the other meaning, which signifies an experiential quality of something
that has been "lived through" by a person.

This non-empiricist understanding of experience survived especially in the domain of theology, where experience has mainly been examined as *religious* (or even spiritual or mystical) experience. In general,
"experience" has been much more essential to religious studies than to
philosophy: academic philosophers seemingly feared to transgress the
limits separating experience from "mystical experience" because philosophy itself was unable to mark these limits clearly. Philosophers who dealt
with experience often decided to approach it from a theological angle. So
did Schleiermacher, the immediate predecessor of Dilthey in his *Über die
Religion* (Schleiermacher 1799). So did the only other Twentieth Century
philosophers who, apart from Dilthey, wrote major books on the problem
of experience: William James in his *The Varieties of Religious Experience*
(1902), and Joachim Wach in his *Typen Religiöser Anthropologie: Eine
vergleichende Lehre vom Menschen im religionsphilosophische Denken
von Okzident und Orient* (1932).[2] Certainly, in the twentieth, century
German hermeneutics' specialized philosophical discourses on the
phenomenon of "Verstehen" (understanding) also included reflections on
"experience," though only to a limited extent. It is also true that, after
Dilthey, Heidegger (and later Gadamer) reevaluated experience as a dynamic phenomenon.[3] In general, however, one can agree with Robert

Experience paralleling
Phenomenology.

Sharf that in Western philosophy as much as in Western religion, experience itself (that is, psychic experience as a personally lived phenomenon) has relatively rarely been the subject of investigation and therefore even until this day remains "obscure" (cf. Sharf 1998: 94).

It remains to be added that this obscurity was even more pronounced during the first three decades of the twentieth century, the time when Sesemann developed his ideas. At that time, psychic experience became more and more "objective" and measurable through the work of the psychology and psychoanalysis of the day. Criticism was uttered only much later by Binswanger (Binswanger 1953) (Bakhtin's case is discussed in the present book) and still later by Lacan (see Chapter 3).

Sharf's criticism is directed towards *"Western"* philosophy. He notes that eastern religions are, in general, more "experientially rooted" and states that "while the emphasis on experience is relatively new in the West, this is clearly not the case in the East" (Sharf 1998: 98). Sharf concludes that corresponding philosophical developments in the "East" are often marked by a more "experiential" tendency.

Should one thus look towards "the East" in order to find parallels with Sesemann? Sesemann adhered to certain parts of the Eurasian culturology and was also very interested in Russian orthodox tradition. Could ways of thinking subsisting outside Western mainstream models have influenced Sesemann's untypical reasoning about experience?

Certain points make me inclined to think so. It cannot be a coincidence that the thinker who most strikingly resembles Sesemann is the Japanese psychologist Kimura Bin (born in 1931) who develops his thoughts in proximity with religion. Tracing all the connections between East and West could fill an entire book. In this introduction I would simply like to point out the striking parallelism between Sesemann's thought and the writings of Kimura Bin who has written passages that almost overlap with those of Sesemann. Kimura recognizes that in Westerns schools of psychotherapy, psychic experience represents a verbalizable experience and "even non-verbal phenomena like dreams [and] transfers [...] can be entered into the field of psychotherapy, to the extent, in which they can be translated into words either by the patient himself or by the therapist" (Kimura 1991: 199). Kimura regrets that in conventional psychoanalysis the patient is obliged to *make his consciousness an object* (200) in order to construct psychic life and dreams.

For Kimura, psychic experiences or events should not be verbalized. Like Sesemann, Kimura discusses these fundamental ideas along the lines of a reflection on "self-perception" (*jikaku*), which is declared the original place of human existence. Exactly like Sesemann, Kimura believes that only in self-perception, man resists all "objectification" of psychic life (Kimura 1992: 40).[4]

The insistence on experience, and the refusal of any objectifying logic underlying experience, appears in several non-Western philosophical traditions including the Upanishadic tradition, but also in medieval Christian mysticism (which dealt with "non-objective logic" through the *via negativa*). Because these traditions are more "experiential," experience and the logic of experience are depicted in another way. Another branch of non-Western philosophy resembles Sesemann's work still more closely: Russian philosophy dependent on the Orthodox tradition. It is particularly interesting to understand this philosophy in the context of "Eastern ideas" (in the largest sense of the term) mentioned above.

Berdiaev's suggestions about the "meonic" which Sesemann adopted (see Appendix I, note 4) are strongly influenced by Jacob Böhme's thoughts about the *Ungrund* (cf. Berdiaev 1930), but they also strike one as immediately related to Sesemann's project. For Berdiaev, the *meonic* represents a "nothingness" in the sense of *me on*. This meonic *Ungrund* is irrational, free and full of potential (because it is not yet determined by God) and thus not objectified. It is an experience that is not yet present "as something" but out of which "something" will be created. James Scanlan comments on Berdiaev's philosophy like this: "The estrangement of man from the world is to a very large extent effectuated through such an abstraction from the (co-conscious), concrete, subjective contents of psychic life; and it always functions – though in a hidden way – through a scientific objectification."[5] The meonic reality of experience should not be objectified; objectification will lead to "estrangement." Is it possible to find a better summary of Sesemann's thoughts on this topic? Sesemann's philosophy, though often technical and linked to the jargon of the Western philosophy of his time, should perhaps be read keeping these "non-Western" ideas in mind.

I would also like to thank the following journals for having granted the permission to reprint revised versions of their articles: *Essays in Poetics* for Chapter 3 that has initially been published in their October 2000 issue; and the *Slavic and East European Journal* for Chapters 1 and 2 that have initially been published in 2003 in their number 46:4. I am also very much indebted to Sesemann's nephew, the late Oscar Parland (1912–1997) and Sesemann's late wife Wilma. I express my thanks to Hermann Parland (Helsinki) who provided an huge amount of supplementary biographical information on Sesemann, and Sesemann's sons Georgijus Sesemanas (Vilnius) and the translator Dimitri Sesemann whom I met in Paris in 1997.

Notes

1. "Über gegenständliches und ungegenständliches Wissen" (Kaunas: Lietuvos universiteto Humaitariu mokslu fakultetu rastai, 1927), p. 95.

2. Tübingen: Mohr, 1932. Engl. trans. in 1951 as *Types of Religious Experience – Christian and Non-Christian*.

3. In *Unterwegs zur Sprache* Heidegger writes: "Mit etwas, sei es ein Ding, ein Mensch, ein Gott, eine Erfahrung machen heisst, dass es uns widerfährt, dass es uns trifft, über uns kommt, uns umwirft und verwandelt" (Frankfurt, Klostermann: 1959, 159). See also Heidegger's "Hegels Begriff der Erfahrung" in *Holzwege* (Klostermann, 1952) and *Aus der Erfahrung des Denkens* (Pfullingen: Neske, 1954).

4. Kimura develops his thoughts on the ground provided by Japan's foremost main philosopher of the twentieth century, Kitaro Nishida. Nishida himself is fundamentally critical of any "objectifying logic" (by which Nishida means mainly Kantian logic). In Nishida's philosophy the refusal of "objectification" of experience is central

5. In Edie, Scanlan & Zeldin: *Russian Philosophy* Vol. III (Knoxville: University of Tennessee Press, 1976), p. 151.

Chapter 1

Sesemann's Life and Work

Vasily Sesemann (1884–1963) is difficult to introduce. The spelling of his name already causes problems because it exists in several national versions. It is Wilhelm (Vilhelm) or Wassily Sesemann in German, Vasilii Emilievich Sezeman in Russian, and Vosylius Sezemanas in Lithuanian. I would like to introduce him as one of such half-forgotten Russian philosophers as S. L. Frank (1877–1950), Gustav Shpet (1879–1937), or Fedor Stepun (1884–1965).[1] For the most part of his life Sesemann was working in a provincial milieu. His philosophical heritage has since long been recognized in Lithuania where his *Estetika* was published in the 1970s and has been regularly used since then as a textbook at universities, and where his *Collected Works* have been edited in 2 volumes between 1987 and 1997 (and been complemented by other editions; see Parland 85, Tarasti "Introduction"). His name is found in newer Russian encyclopedias; in the West, however, he remains rather unknown. Sesemann has had considerable problems with the Soviet regime, and ended up in a Siberian labor camp at the peak of his career. Thus one has good reason to suppose that some of his significant thoughts never had the chance to be appreciated by the larger public.

Vyborg around 1920

If he needs to be labeled it would be easiest to label him a "Baltic philosopher" or, if one prefers the more complicated option, as a Finnish-Russian-German-Lithuanian philosopher. In some way, his personality symbolizes the coherence of Baltic culture, which implies, for good or bad, the lack of any real national identity. What makes Sesemann's case even more difficult is the fact that he decided to publish in several languages. In general, multi-language authors like Sesemann are reserved for highly specialized circles because cultural barriers and linguistic barriers render them inaccessible to potential readers. His Lithuanian writings are read only by a small minority of people, and his Russian and German output risks falling between the camps of scholars of German and of Russian philosophy respectively, between whom needed communication is not always to be found.

Sesemann with mother and sister in 1926

In historical terms, Sesemann's multicultural background makes him extraordinary. Raised in Vyborg and St. Petersburg in a traditional German-Lutheran home, Sesemann maintained a remarkable interest in Russian culture throughout his lifetime, including a fascination with the Russian Orthodox Church. Given his German background, the motives for this might appear obscure. The same is true for Sesemann's involvement with the so-called "Eurasian Movement," – an emigrant movement from the 1920s on, which sees Russia's historical position as that of a unique "Eurasian" cultural community, fundamentally distinct from European as well as Asian culture. His Eurasian engagement might give rise to much speculation, but it will probably be impossible to obtain a clear concept of the links between these activities and his academic writing.

Given the relative obscurity of Sesemann's biography, the historical Vasily Sesemann will not be the subject of the present study. Its aim is rather to show that Sesemann produced ideas that appear unique within the Russian and Baltic environment of his time and that these ideas are interesting even within contemporary discussions of philosophy and psychology.

Sesemann was born in 1884 in the then Finnish, now Russian town of Vyborg.[2] His father Emil Hermann (1840-1907), also born in Vyborg, was a doctor of German descent who had studied in Vienna, and had lectured on anatomy at the University of Helsinki. At the time of Vasily's birth, he was working as a railway doctor for the Finnish Railway Administration, practicing on the St. Petersburg-Vyborg line.

Sesemann's mother Ida Maria (nee Baekmann) was the daughter of a Baltic-German minister from Livland. Her religious faith as well as her German patriotism were rather intense and seem to have been somewhat in contrast to the scientific rationalism of his father. Sesemann later held that the tension between both poles had been very important for his early intellectual development.[3]

Historical records mention the name Sesemann among those German families who arrived in Vyborg in the second half of the seventeenth century to engage in the wood and paper business (Schweizer: 29ff.). The fact that the Sesemanns, in spite of the long-lasting geographical separation from the *Reich*, still spoke German at home should not be seen as something unusual. This was common for German

minorities that were distributed all over Eastern Europe before World War II. Especially in Vyborg there was a relatively large German-speaking minority.[4] After the unification of the German provinces, German culture and German national symbols were even more highly valued in these German *"Randgebiete"* by their German speaking residents. Especially in the Lutheran Baltikum a strong pro-German attitude was common among the middle class and was even intensified by the relatively strict separation that existed between the social classes.

Memorial stone in Hanko

Sesemann grew up in St. Petersburg, where his parents had been living since 1871, though they usually spent their holidays and weekends in Vyborg. In St. Petersburg he attended the German Katharinen-Schule that had been founded by his grandfather, the Reverend Boekmann. According to his classmate and longtime friend, the Formalist and specialist in same institution, pupils there received a "thoroughly classical" education (Zhirmunsky: 3).

From 1903 to 1909 Sesemann studied at the University of St. Petersburg, first for two semesters at the Faculty of Medicine in order to become a doctor like his farther, and then at the Faculty of History and Philosophy where he received degrees in philosophy and philology in 1914. Among his teachers was the Russian intuitive philosopher N. O. Lossky (1870–1965), who exercised a significant influence on him. In 1914 Sesemann received his Master Degree for a dissertation on *The Philosophy of Gymnastics*. For the rest of his life, he intensively practiced gymnastics and remained particularly interested in the philosophical aspects of this discipline, one of which is certainly that of "rhythm."

From 1909 to 1911 Sesemann studied in Marburg, Germany, where the philosophy department represented the "Marburg School" of Neo-Kantianism. At first sight, this seems to create a strong link between Sesemann and other Russian philosophers who studied at the same time under German Neo-Kantians, for example Fedor Stepun (who was, like Sesemann, born in 1884 into a German-speaking family involved in the paper production) or Sergei Gessen (1887–1950). However, Sesemann never met these Russians because they studied in Heidelberg, absorbing the teachings of the Southwest German Neo-Kantian School built around the personality of Windelband.[5]

Still, Marburg was full of other interesting foreigners, many of them Russians. Sesemann met Ortega y Gasset by whom he was very much impressed, and Sergei S. Oldenburg, the later Ultramonarchist who emigrated to Paris and son of the famous Russian indologist.[6] The most important fact about Sesemann's Marburg time is, however, that here he consolidated his lifelong friendship with Nicolai Hartmann (1882–1950).

Sesemann practicing gymnastics

Hartmann, a Riga-born Baltic-German, was two years older than Sesemann and had arrived in Marburg already in 1905. Sesemann and Hartmann had attended the German Middleschool in St. Petersburg and studied philosophy at the University. It was Hartmann who persuaded Sesemann to switch from medicine to philosophy. Hartmann became Professor of Philosophy in Marburg in 1920 and is now recognized as an important German Prewar philosopher. Sesemann's and Hartmann's relationship remained close during their lifetimes. Hartmann visited Sesemann several times in Finland, both married Russian women, and it was Hartmann who recommended Sesemann for the newly created post at the University of Kaunas. In Marburg, both friends attended the lectures of Cohen and Natorp. Both would never study under the third main figure of the Marburg School, Ernst Cassirer, because Cassirer was teaching in Berlin by 1906.[7]

Upon his return to St. Petersburg,[8] Sesemann taught philosophy and classical languages at high school until the outbreak of World War I, after which he was a volunteer in the Russian army (from 1914 to 1915). From 1915 to 1917 he taught philosophy as a *Privatdozent* at the University of St. Petersburg, and from 1918 to 1919 at the Viatka Pedagogical Institute. He received a "docentship" in Saratov, where, together with Zhirmunsky, he worked until 1921.[9]

The friction between Finland and Russia (by which he could have been affected as a Finnish citizen), or even more the bad material conditions in Petrograd, forced him to move to Finland. He went there with his wife Antonina Nikolaevna and their sons in November 1921 (their second son Dimitri was born in Helsinki in January 1922). The Karelian uprising in winter 1922 made any return to Russia impossible. Unable to find work in Finland (apparently the University of Helsinki was unwilling to recognize his Russian doctorate),[10] he went for one year (from May 1922 to June 1923) to Berlin where first he had a variety of odd jobs but finally found a teaching position at the Russian Institute. (He could not meet Cassirer then either because Cassirer had left Berlin just a year before for Hamburg.) In Berlin he frequented Berdiaev's Eurasian circle and in March 1923 would participate, together with Berdiaev, S. L. Frank, B.N. Vysheslavtsev, F.A. Stepun, S.I. Gessen, G.G. Kulman and Paul Tillich, in a public discussion organized by Berdiaev's Academy of Spiritual Culture whose subject was the philosophy of Max Scheler.[11]

Sesemann left Berlin the moment he received a post as Professor of Aesthetics at the newly founded University of Kaunas in Lithuania. He stayed in Lithuania, moving in 1940, together with the university, from Kaunas to Vilnius. (The Vilnius area had until 1920 been occupied by Poland and was only in 1939 definitely integrated into the Soviet Union; at that moment the university was removed from the temporary capital Kaunas to Vilnius).[12] In 1923 Sesemann became Professor of Logic and Aesthetics in Kaunas. He learned the Lithuanian language relatively quickly and already in 1929 published his 304-page *Logika* in Lithuanian.

The Sesemann property in Tikala (now Russia)

The most important and also closest acquaintance from Sesemann's time in Kaunas and Vilnius is certainly that with the Russian historian and philosopher Lev Platonovich Karsavin (1882–1952). Karsavin, opposed to the Revolution, had to emigrate in 1920 to Berlin where he was associated with Berdiaev's Academy. This is where Sesemann and Karsavin met. Later, it was through Sesemann's recommendation that in 1929 Karsavin received a professorship, first at Kovno and then at Vilnius University in Art History and Aesthetics.[13]

In Vilnius, both philosophers would occupy pleasant apartments in the Radzivilsky Palace. Karsavin integrated into Lithuanian intellectual life even faster than Sesemann and learned Lithuanian with unusual speed. Both appreciated living close to Russia, and Karsavin later declined a position at Oxford University for that reason. Sesemann also decided not to leave Vilnius even when Soviet troops invaded the city in 1944, which can be seen as an unusual decision, given that his second wife was of German origin.[14]

Because Karsavin opposed the Soviet occupation of Lithuania, he lost his position in 1945 (but he could keep his apartment). He was arrested about a year before Sesemann and died in 1952 in the Abeza camp north of the polar circle in the Autonomous Republic of Komi. As a historian, Karsavin took Orthodox belief as a framework for his research and was active in the Eurasian movement. Of course, Sesemann had been initiated to Eurasianism already before his time in Berlin. His wife Antonina Nikolaeva Nasonova (from whom Sesemann got divorced in 1923) was active in the Eurasian movement up to the point when she had to leave Paris in 1937 in order to avoid inspections by the French security service, the "Sureté." Trying to hide in the Soviet Union, she was nevertheless arrested in 1939 and sentenced to death in 1941 for "collaboration with the Eurasian movement."

The Sesemann-Parland family in Tikala

Against this background, Sesemann's own Eurasian aspirations appear rather modest. In 1925 he published an article in the Parisian Eurasian journal *Evraziiskii Vremionnik*. The content of the article "Socrates and the Problem of Self-Knowledge" cannot be called "Eurasian" as such, though it can be read, in the context in which it was published as a Eurasian philosophical statement. Sesemann traces the typically European striving of knowledge (with its optimism, intellectualism, theoretical penchant, etc.) back to Socrates and shows that, because European civilization has so far been unwilling to change its course, a major civilizational crisis is unavoidable. A "Eurasian way" as an alternative able to triumph over decadent European culture is not spelled out by Sesemann but was certainly implicit for "Eurasian" readers.[15] In the 1930s, Sesemann's ex-wife and sons lived in Paris while he was in Lithuania. Far from being isolated in a belated Neo-Kantian enclosure, Sesemann maintained direct contact with European intellectual life.[16] He usually went to Paris twice a year, in summer and at Christmas, to spend time with his sons. Around 1933 he could regularly be found in Berdiaev's milieu, which now contained mainly the same people that Sesemann already knew from his time in Berlin: Karsavin, Ilin, Zak, and, according to the MGB protocol, the eminent Eurasianist and Karsavin's son-in-law, Petr Nikolaevich Suvchinsky.[17] Sesemann also frequently visited

Leningrad and Moscow to try to keep up with Russia's latest intellectual developments.

A last wave of the "campaign against formalism"[17] (which began in the 1920s), put an end to all this. Since 1947 Sesemann had occupied the chair of philosophy at the University of Vilnius. He lost his position in 1949 and was replaced by a philosopher chosen by the party. Defending his case in Moscow, he was assigned a post at the University of Minsk. With the railway tickets for Minsk in his pocket, he saw police officials searching his flat until they found certain Eurasian journals that Sesemann had received from Karsavin's eldest daughter Irina. In 1950, at the age of 66, Sesemann was arrested for "anti-Soviet activities" and sent to a labor camp in Taishet (Irkutsk) for fifteen years. Karsavin's daughter Irina was deported soon after.

The reasons for Sesemann's arrest cannot be entirely established. The protocols of the MGB clearly put forward his Eurasian activities and contacts with emigrants, and insist heavily on his relationship with Karsavin. The Eurasian case seems to make sense in light of the fate of Sesemann's wife. At the same time however, it must be said that Eurasianism as such was no longer considered an anti-Soviet activity and the MGB argumentation may look like pretext. Certainly, as a former Finnish subject (contrary to what is written in most sources, Sesemann had already adopted Soviet citizenship in 1941, not just after his release from prison), Sesemann was looked at with a critical eye. Though he was, generally, loyal towards the regime, he may have made critical remarks from time to time; nor was the fact that he continuously entertained contacts with suspicious "formalists" as well as with Jews unimportant.

L.P. Karsavin

It is uncertain what has happened to some of Sesemann's manuscripts. According to Sesemann's second wife Wilma, a number of manuscripts had been placed on a rug at the moment of his arrest and were subsequently burned outside of his house.[19] However, other manuscripts had been hidden by friends and were returned to Sesemann upon his release. The *Estetika* manuscript, for example, had been hidden for many years in a shed in the countryside before being published in the 1970s. While it is uncertain whether his manuscripts were really burned, his entire library was taken from his house, and the largest part of it has never reappeared.

In the camp, Sesemann was forced to do physical labor for a considerable amount of time. He was set free in 1956 under the Khrushchev regime, and in 1958 returned to his former position at Vilnius University. Sesemann died in 1963.

Thomas Nemeth, in his "Russian Neo-Kantianism" entry in the *Routledge Encyclopedia of Philosophy*, presents a rather negative image of Sesemann as one of the "last Russian Neo-Kantians" (together with the elderly Vvedensky, Chelpanov, and the Latvian Veidemann).[20] Sesemann, Nemeth writes, "perhaps alone among the Neo-Kantians in the Russian Diaspora, continued working without thematic abatement on problems traditionally conceived as philosophical, keeping abreast of the latest developments."[21] The isolationist scheme is overstated not only in light of Sesemann's regular contacts with Elitist emigrant circles, but also with regard to him as the philosopher who wrote the first Russian review article on Heidegger in 1928.[22] In this context, Sesemann is indeed closer to S.I. Gessen and even more to F.A. Stepun, both of whom touched upon Neo-Kantian ideas in their youth, and who, having been exposed to many other influences, "worked out a theory of their own" (Lossky, *Istoriia russkoi filosofii*: 402) in their later years.

Adopting this perspective, it is possible to identify some of Sesemann's main philosophical tendencies that had been created within a unique Baltic climate traditionally determined by a strong tension between Russian and Germanic culture. Sesemann's critical relationship with Neo-Kantianism caused him to react in a particular way not only to Russian Formalism but also, *together with* the Russian Formalists, to Russian intuitivism and related movements. Zhirmunsky's affirmation of Sesemann's Formalist connection, written for the preface of Sesemann's *Estetika* (and available only in Lithuanian), is understood in this light:

> He always followed discussions in literature, especially Russian Formalist theoretical works which he admired, but which he also criticized fundamentally. He was mainly looking for support in Broder Christiansen's *Philosophy of Art* (translated into Russian in 1911), especially in his theory of the dominant and "differential impression" [*Differenzimpression*] and their role in the development of art (later those concepts were adopted by other literary theoreticians, for example by Y. Tynianov) (Zhirmunsky: 5).[23]

In his *History of Russian Philosophy*, Nicolas Lossky dedicates three pages to Sesemann and includes him not in the chapter on Neo-Kantianism but in that group of the Russian philosophers who "поддержали контакт с немецкой философей послекантовского периода" ["kept contact with

German post-Kantian philosophy"] (405).[24] Lossky names this group the "Transcendental-Logical Idealists," a name that deserves attention. The young Russian philosophers Gessen, Stepun, Jakovenko, and (according to Lossky) also Sesemann founded a Russian branch of the international journal *Logos*. However, for Lossky this "transcendental-logical-idealism" seems to be a kind of "freestyle derivative" of Neo-Kantianism, at its root incompatible with original Kantian motives. Beyond that, it had not been invented by these young Russians, but was already fully developed in Germany by that time. For Lossky, Rickert, Cohen and Natorp are not Neo-Kantians, due to their rejection of any psychological arguments within the theory of knowledge, which makes their philosophies fundamentally non-Kantian as such. Hence, Lossky calls their philosophies "logical-transcendental."[25]

Lossky's judgment is certainly tendentious and distorts the history of Neo-Kantianism. However, for these young Russians themselves, though often identified with a new brand of Russian Neo-Kantianism, the foundation of the Russian *Logos* itself was an even more "open" phenomenon than "transcendental-logical idealism." (Stepun [97, 130] describes how the journal was founded in Rickert's Heidelberg apartment and how the original, not at all Neo-Kantian sounding title "Of Messiah" [Über Messias] aroused Windelband's cynical criticism.)[26] It is better to say that Sesemann was active within a circle of young Russian philosophers who insisted neither very much on their Neo-Kantian, nor on their "idealist" orientation. Their approach was rather, in an eclectic or sometimes even paradoxical way, a mixed Eastern-Western one that included – and here Lossky's insight is indeed penetrating – too many "intuitive procedures" in itself that it could still be considered real "Kantianism" (Sesemann's later affinities with Bergson certainly testify to this). Widening the circle of these "open Neo-Kantians," one can even include people like Georges D. Gurvitch (whom Lossky links to Sesemann) and (if one drops the "intuitive" charge) Gustav Shpet.[27]

It remains to say that Sesemann's label as a "transcendental-logical idealist," which he received from his master, could also push him (though certainly this is not what Lossky meant) in the direction of people whom he also did not oppose, i.e. the real "idealists": Solovyov's followers Pavel Florensky, Sergei Bulgakov, S. L. Frank, and Karsavin. In reality, however, Sesemann's relationship with the Russian "Idealist tradition" is as ambiguous as his relationship with Realism. His case is complex. To show the full breadth of the spectrum, one can mention that Sesemann's concern for especially formal questions in linguistics and aesthetics even makes him, for some people, a precursor of modern semiotics (Parland: 85 and Tarasti).

Instead of classifying him, it is best to regard Sesemann as a mirror reflecting the confusing situation in Europe, which, during the first three decades of the twentieth century, had an impact on even basic philosophical concepts. Sesemann found an admirable way to bring order into this chaotic situation. His philosophy establishes a link between the standard Formalist problem of the "dynamization of the structure" and a concept of Being that, to postwar readers, must be (like Nicolai Hartmann's) reminiscent of Heidegger. In this way his philosophy has a real European flavor of comprehensiveness.

By and large, Sesemann wrote as much in Russian as he had in German and, at a later stage of his life, had also been able to write and teach in Lithuanian.[28] Certainly, the inaccessibility of his Lithuanian writings makes overall appreciation of his work very difficult. It is particularly regrettable that the *Estetika*, a posthumously published collection of his essays and lectures on aesthetics, though generally considered one of his most important works, is only available in Lithuanian. Moreover, Sesemann published very little, and (apart from the Lithuanian *Logika* and a volume of "lectures" [*paskaitos*]) he published not a single book, though he certainly had enough material to put into book form. Hartmann does his best, in a review article, by treating Sesemann's two articles (linked through the common heading "Die logischen Gesetze und das Sein" and published in 1931 in the same volume of *Eranos)*, to act as if together they were a book.[29] Indeed, the articles fill 170 pages and look like a book manuscript published in two parts in a journal.

The same is true for another series of articles. Sesemann's originality appears most clearly in three articles published between 1927 and 1930, dedicated to the problem of *Erkenntnis*, or to the problem of *knowledge* as it appears in German *Erkenntnistheorie*.[30] The three articles appeared in two different journals; however all shared the heading "Beiträge zum Erkenntnisproblem" [Contributions to the Problem of Knowledge], and developed different aspects of that theme. The first two of these articles, published in consecutive numbers of *Kaunas University Humanities Department Annals* in the same year, appear much like a book, together representing 138 pages. If one adds the third "part" (which differs slightly in focus but is still similar), the trilogy can easily be considered a book of roughly 200 pages.

These two series of articles could thus be considered to be Sesemann's two main works. They are also arguably the most substantial of Sesemann's writings with regard to contents and originality. Before 1935, that is between 1911 and 1925, Sesemann published eleven articles, eight of which are in Russian and three in German. Two of these articles clearly prepare the themes that are to reappear in the "books" mentioned, which are "rhythm" and "self-perception." Between 1935 and 1961 there are no publications in Russian or German but only in Lithuanian (Sesemann was arrested in 1950).

After his release from the prison camp Sesemann worked mainly on logic.

There are no more publications in German, and his only publication in Russian from the short period between his release from prison and his death, is an article called "Pustye i universal'nye klassy sovremennoj logike," published in 1962. Apart from that, there are still five unpublished Russian manuscripts and typescripts, for the largest part dealing with the subject of logic, including the 95-page text "Logika," which is probably related to his 304-page Lithuanian *Logika* published in 1929 in Vilnius.

Sesemann's highly productive period for texts accessible to non-Lithuanian readers, has been between 1911 and 1935 – a period during which he published 21 articles including the "book-like" ones previously discussed. Sesemann's most creative period – in terms of both quantity and originality – falls between 1925 and 1931.

Nina Nassonov, Sesemann's first wife

Sesemann translated two works: Lossky's *Logika* into German published in 1922 which might be the only work by Sesemann distributed on an international level (see note 25), and Aristotle's *On the Soul* into Lithuanian, done in the prison camp and published in 1959. According to some sources, Sesemann did not have Aristotle's original in the camp but knew it by heart.

The following chapter of the present book will not deal with Sesemann's "books." In Chapter 3 I will show that Sesemann's critique of the Freudian "materialization" (*Vergegenständlichung*) of psychic life (present especially in the first part of the "trilogy" "Beiträge zum Erkenntnisproblem") is not only reminiscent of Voloshinov and Bakhtin, but also of contemporary Freudian criticism offered by Lacan, thoughts which appear mainly in the two "books." However, in the same year in which the first two parts of Sesemann's trilogy were published, an interesting article appears by him in Russian, called "Iskusstvo i kul'tura" [k probleme estetika]; ("Art and Culture: The Problem of Aesthetics").

In this article, Sesemann addresses similar ideas, but now links them, among other things, to "Formalism." The subject of the following chapter will mainly focus on the internal implications of "Iskusstvo i kul'tura."

Old Kaunas

Notes

1. Sesemann's philosophy should arouse interest also in the light of recent publications on similar authors: A new article on S. L. Frank's Neo-Kantian links by P. Swoboda and a new book on Fedor Stepun by Christian Hufen. Comparisons of Sesemann and Frank would perhaps be fruitful, because both had a common heritage of Lossky and H. Cohen. Apart from that, they also share a common interest in Bergson (cf. last chapter). Also Shpet's work is widely studied by international phenomenologists. Recent translation: Shpet, *Appearance and Sense*.

2. For basic biographical facts about Sesemann mainly see the entry "Sezemanas (Sezeman, Sesemann)" of the *Encyclopedia Lithaunica* (Boston, 1976 Vol. 5), 126–127 (which contains some errors), and a book by Sesemann's nephew, the Finnish writer Oscar Parland (1912–1997), which contains a chapter on Sesemann. For more precise biographical information I am very much indebted to Hermann Parland (Helsinki), and Sesemann's sons Georg Sezemanas (Vilnius) and Dimitri Sesemann (Paris), as well as to Sesemann's late wife Wilma.

3. Sesemann's father is said to have volunteered for several months as a sanitation worker in the German-French war in 1870–71 for the Prussian army due to the persuasion of his pro-German wife. His mother's veneration for the German emperor also inspired Sesemann's first name "Wilhelm" which he seems to have disliked. On most occasions he later changed it to "Wassily."

4. Even today in the Baltic region one can find descendants from Vyborg Germans who testify to having grown up in a quatri-lingual (Russian, German, Finnish and Swedish) environment. Being raised mainly in St. Petersburg, Sesemann learned neither Finnish nor Swedish in his early youth, but took Swedish lessons later in Vyborg because he believed it to be necessary to speak at least one of the languages of one's "home country." He later spoke and wrote Swedish fluently.

5. This is of importance because of the difference between the Southwest German school of Neo-Kantianism (Windelband, Rickert, Lask) and the Marburg School (represented by Cohen, Natorp, and Cassirer). Around 1910 Rickert's philosophy was certainly most important in Russia for pre-Formalist trends of thought and was propagated by A. Vvedensky in his philosophy lectures at St. Petersburg University. Gessen was most influenced by Rickert through his studies in Heidelberg. Stepun never studied with Rickert, because Rickert arrived in Heidelberg only in 1916. Later, Gessen, together with D. H. Kogen and P. B. Struve, would enter the 2nd group of the R.F.O. (*Russkoe Filosofskoe Obshestvo*) of St. Petersburg. See J. Scherrer 308ff, and works by Russian Neo-Kantians: Gessen: *Individuelle Kausalität*, and "Novyi opyt;" Vvedensky.

6. Ortega y Gasset (1883–1955) was no longer a regular student in Marburg but had studied in Marburg and Berlin between 1898 and 1902, and received his Ph.D. in 1904 from

the University of Madrid. Sergei S. Oldenburg, son of the indologist S. F. Oldenburg (1863–1934), later lived in Paris and wrote a biography of Nicolas II. Sesemann might also have met the important Polish aesthetician Wladylav Tatarkiewicz (1886–1979) who studied in Marburg and Berlin from 1905 to 1910 and received his Ph.D. from the University of Marburg in 1910.

7. Cassirer had become a *Privatdozent* in Berlin in 1906. Theoretically Hartmann could have attended Cassirer's lectures in Marburg for one year, but Cassirer's influence on Hartmann remained limited. Sesemann would not meet Boris Pasternak (1890–1960) in Marburg either, since Pasternak (who also studied philosophy) arrived in Marburg only in 1912, one year after Sesemann had left. Hartmann was still in Marburg in the 1920s and must have met Pasternak at that time. Nor did Sesemann meet another Marburg icon, Karl Barth, who was absent from Marburg between 1909 and 1911.

8. Some sources, for example Zhirmunsky in his preface to Sesemann's *Estetika*, hold that, before going home to St. Petersburg, Sesemann went to Berlin in 1911 after his Marburg stay. This seems to be likely, but it is not known whom he met at that time in Berlin.

9. Semyon L. Frank held a professorship in Saratov after the revolution, but it is not known if Sesemann and Frank met prior to their meeting in Berlin in 1922.

10. The Department of Philosophy at the University of Helsinki emphasized teaching on "Logical Empiricism" and the Vienna Circle, a tendency which Sesemann, who came straight out of a Russian education oriented towards classical humanism, rejected at that time as well as later in his life.

11. The discussion took place on March 18, 1923. See K. Schlögel et. al. 169.

12. Quarrels between Poland and Lithuania led in 1920 to the Polish control of the Vilnius territory, and the University of Vilnius was removed to the temporary capital Kaunas. A new Polish university was founded in Wilno in 1921. In September 1939, Russian troops occupied Lithuania (it was actually no real occupation but part of a mutual assistance pact; the occupation happened one year later). Though Lithuania was not immediately integrated into the Soviet Union, the capital was returned to Lithuania. Immediately the University was moved back to Vilnius and installed on the premises of the former Stefan Batory University, or, as others see it, the University of Wilno was "lithuanianized."

13. Evidence of a close friendship between Sesemann and Karsavin is also provided by letters from Sesemann's nephew, the Finnish Futurist poet Henry Parland, who lived with Sesemann during these years in Kaunas. See Per Stam's thesis on Henry Parland and the Appendix IV.

14. In a book that was published in 1978 by Vilnius University on the occasion of its 400th anniversary, it is documented that Prof. Sesemann had helped, along with others, to put out the fire at the University, kindled by the retreating Germans, and thus he helped to save the university.

15. In his book on Eurasianism, Böss sees Sesemann's article as a philosophical foundation of Eurasian ideology. Otto Böss: *Die Lehre der Eurasier* (Wiesbaden: Harrassowitz, 1961), p. 77.

16. For a long time it has been unknown which emigrants Sesemann had actually met there. Now, however, the protocols of the MGB (Ministry of State Control, *Ministerstvo gosudarstvenoi bezopasnosti*) are accessible, and from these protocols we learn that Sesemann met not only Ivan Ilin and Semyon Frank, but also the painter Lev Zak (S. Frank's step brother), and a certain Goseion (*Narodnii Kommisariat Vnutrennikh Del*, entry from October 1, 1946). In Paris he probably also met the writer Aleksei Remizov (1877–1957), who had emigrated to Paris in 1924. A postcard from Sesemann can be found in Remizov's correspondence. (The sources are two MGB documents, the first one is titled "Memorandum" from July 1944; the second one is titled "Spravka," dated 1948. No other numbers can be seen on the documents.)

17. Petr Nikolaevitch Suvchinsky organized the Eurasian movement from about 1923 together with Prince N.S Trubetzkoy, P.N. Savitsky, and G.V. Florovsky.

18. According to Oscar Parland, who bases his statements on personal talks that he has had with his uncle, an anti-Formalist campaign was responsible for Sesemann's arrest.

19. This event is also described in his thesis by Per Stam, who received the information from Sesemann's wife. Oscar Parland's account of the destiny of the books and manuscripts is a little different. According to him, the books were taken away in a bag by the police at the moment of Sesemann's arrest. A combined version of both accounts might come close to the truth.

20. Sesemann wrote an "Introduction" to Alexander Veidemann's book *Предмед Познания: Основная Часть (Мышление и Бытие)* (Riga: Sfinkss, 1937).

21. Nemeth's entry-article contains an interesting interpretation of Sesemann's early philosophy from a Neo-Kantian point of view.

22. In the late 1950s Sesemann got hold of Wittgenstein's *Philosophische Unter-suchung* which made him enthusiastic because this was "finally different from the Tractatus" (Letter to Hermann Parland).

23. Broder Christiansen (1969–1958): *Philosophie der Kunst* (Hanau: Claus & Feddersen, 1909). Sesemann discusses Christiansen's theory of *Stimungsimpressionen* and *Differentials* in his article "O prirode poeticheskogo obrasa" (1925), part of which are presented in the present volume in the Appendix II.

24. Among bibliographical essays on Sesemann there is also a 1995 article by A. Konitzky entitled "Vasily Seseman" in *Vil'nius* Nr. 4 (143), pp. 123–130 (in Russian).

25. Lossky develops an interesting criticism of this form of "Kantianism" in the article in which he analyses many of those arguments that were also Sesemann's: "Fichtes konkrete Ethik."

26. See also C H. Besrodny.

27. The French sociologist Georgii Davidovitch Gurvitch (1894–1965) was born in Russia, studied Law and Philosophy in Petrograd from 1912 to 1917 and was Assistant Professor at Petrograd University during 1918. According to Lossky, he had been attracted in his youth by "transcendental-logical idealism," which brought him in contact with Russian Neo-Kantian philosophers. He worked in Tomsk until his emigration to Prague and lived in France from 1921 on, and is today recognized as an eminent French sociologist of Russian origin. Gustav Shpet had also initially been attracted by Neo-Kantian philosophy before abandoning it for phenomenology.

28. Sesemann's most important works in Lithuanian are: *Logika*, *Paskaitos* [Lectures], and *Estetika*. The newly established Lithuanian edition of Sesemann's works consists of two volumes of *Works* [=Rastai]: Vol. 1: *Gnoseologia*; Vol. 2: *Filosofijos istorija.*

29. Reviewed by Hartmann in *Kantstudien* 1931: 227–232. Hartmann's review is reprinted in his *Kleinere Schriften* Bd. 2: 368–374, and there characteristically called "*Buch*besprech-ung" (my italics).

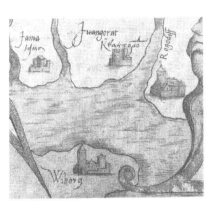

Map of Vyborg in 1540

30. *Erkenntnistheorie* [theory of knowledge] was particularly important in Germany in the middle of the nineteenth century. It is closely linked to the Kantian heritage of the critics

of reason or critics of knowledge [Erkenntniskritik]. Neo-Kantianism (especially Cassirer) developed *Erkenntnistheorie* into an autonomous, non-empirical, scientific discipline.

Chapter 2

Neo-Kantianism, Formalism, and the Question of Being

The purpose of the present chapter is not so much to engage in further comparative research of Sesemann and Bakhtin, or of Sesemann and a later generation of Russian structuralists, such as Yury Lotman (who took note of Sesemann only very late). Nor will Sesemann be presented as a unique link between German Neo-Kantianism and Russian philosophy, or even Neo-Kantianism and Russian Formalism. There were other Russian philosophers who were more outspokenly Neo-Kantian, and there were more who were "Formalists." True, Sesemann focused on themes that are common to Formalists and Neo-Kantians (for Thomas Nemeth he is even the "last representative" of Russian Neo-Kantianism).[1] However, in spite of the timely, geographical, and to some extent intellectual parallels, I believe that he can be compared neither with Formalists like Viktor Shklovsky (1893–1984), Boris Eikhenbaum (1886–1959) and Yury Tynianov (1894–1943), nor with Russian Neo-Kantians like Matvei I. Kagan (1889–1937).[2]

The present chapter attempts to depict the intellectual environment within which Sesemann's original thoughts grew. Of course, given the broad scope of Sesemann's interest, many sources can only be touched upon. I even stop short of systematizing this "broad scope" because I do not know it in its whole breadth, being unable to read the Lithuanian part of Sesemann's œuvre. Beyond that, since Sesemann's life and work is complex, it is difficult to establish a focus for research. Some of his ideas are original and can be very well explained in the context of Bakhtin studies or that of psychoanalysis; the origin of these ideas, however, is to be found in very dispersed sources which – far from being all "Neo-Kantian," "Formalist," or belonging to any other labeled movement – take the researcher at times into completely different fields.

Apart from that, it must be said that to introduce Sesemann as an intellectual innovator runs the risk of passing over the main points of Sesemann's personality. For his contemporaries, Sesemann's real strength did not lay in his spectacular views on certain philosophical subjects, but rather in his painstaking and thorough analyses of difficult philosophical problems.

This is the line that the present book attempts to follow. Sesemann's writings manifest a profound treatment of several questions, which, especially in the first three decades of this century, moved back and forth between Germany and Russia. Taking off one's Neo-Kantian or "Formalist" glasses, one must name these themes in the way that they are named in Sesemann's writings: *empathy* as a model for philosophical *Erkenntnis* [knowledge]; the ambiguity of "form" in aesthetics; the dangers of materialism and positivism for European thought; and, linked to this, the question of the subject in psychology.

1. The Background: Lipps, Lossky and "Formalism"

A. The Ambiguities of Empathy: Gnoseological Idealism

First, it will be necessary to elucidate the background of Sesemann's project since, particularly in his case, too straightforward an analysis of his arguments risks simplification. This is suggested by the fact that one year after the publication of "Iskusstvo i kul'tura," appeared Sesemann's review article of Heidegger's *Sein und Zeit* appeared.[3] Sesemann praises the book as the most important German philosophical work since Scheler. Unfortunately, we do not find more substantial comments on Heidegger in Sesemann however; "Iskusstvo i kul'tura" itself is reminiscent of some Heideggerian themes, as will be shown.

However, before dealing with this article we must elaborate the important link between Sesemann and Nicolai Hartmann (1882–1950), Sesemann's friend from Marburg, who, like Heidegger, abandoned early Neo-Kantian ambitions in order to grasp the foundations of "knowledge (*Erkenntnis*)." Around 1921 Hartmann shifted his concerns from Neo-Kantianism towards questions of ontology.[4] Sesemann's philosophy comes close to what he himself labeled "gnoseological idealism," a term more or less matching the self-definition of philosophical thought to which Hartmann also subscribed.[5] Whereas Neo-Kantianism insists on the *subjectivist* component of metaphysics and tries, by continuing Kantian strategies developed in the nineteenth century, to establish *Erkenntnistheorie* (see note 26) as the successor of metaphysics, Hartmann's philosophy attempts to revive metaphysics through a re-evaluation of the question of Being. Historically, the concern with Being enables Sesemann and Hartmann to resist any temptation to embrace positivism. On this point they are indeed similar to Max Scheler in Germany, and Lossky in Russia.

To understand Sesemann's "gnoseological idealism" one first needs to have a look at the general philosophical discourse of that time. A philosophical problem central to the theory of understanding was the question whether to opt for idealism or realism, or for a possible reconciliation of the two. Scheler has much dealt with this question.[6] There was also, in Germany and Russia, a debate between anti-subjectivism and a philosophy that based its approach on the idea of *Einfühlung* [empathy]. In Germany alone, the problem of *Einfühlung* has a strange and tortuous history covering the entire nineteenth century. It appeared with Herder and Novalis, and developed through the psychologist Theodor Lipps[7] into a process of "identification" objectifying the subject. Bakhtin criticized this idea. More peculiar is the fact that, because of the directness and "avoidance" of rationality within the process of understanding, *Einfühlung* could, at some point, "turn abstract" and lay the foundation for positivism. The fight between anti-subjectivists on the one hand, and subjectivists believing in the importance of *Einfühlung* on the other, thus foreshadows the rise of "logical positivism" which was later going to dominate part of the German scene.

It is certainly no coincidence that in the first two decades of the twentieth century, the central figure philosophizing about the problem of *Einfühlung* was not a philosopher but a psychologist, namely Theodor Lipps.[8] The work of Lipps inspired international discussions concerning the problem of empathy in the theory of knowledge. Lipps drew up a theory of understanding which saw "psychology as a philosophy made scientific" (Lipps: 19), a phrase which itself contains a great deal of the tension that dominated discussion at that time. Psychology itself was rejected by early positivism because it was seen as being derived from Kantian subjectivism. Positivists think that philosophy should be exclusively considered an activity dealing with *objects*, not with the psychological content of the minds of individuals. Thus Lipps's formulation touched a nerve in his time. If psychology is a "scientific philosophy," it must be based on exactly the kind of rationalism that can only be provided by an anti-metaphysical philosophy. But why then should it still be called psychology?

Nicolai Hartmann

The question can be posed in yet another way: *if* psychology (which is originally the discipline dealing with the *subjective* content of the human mind) becomes truly *scientific*, it will finally be able to produce *objective* results. However, if the subjective contents of the human mind is supposed to become objective, should one then rely on a *subjectivist* discipline such as psychology as a means to make it *objective*? This appears paradoxical.

The speculative considerations sketched above involve a focus on the complicated relationships between anti-metaphysical subjectivism (which prepared the ground for logical positivism), and parallel philosophical movements which attempted to re-evaluate philosophical idealism.

Neo-Kantianism was related to this problematic. Neo-Kantianism is complicated and far from straightforward in its development. Since Sesemann's, like Hartmann's links with Neo-Kantianism are relatively loose, I suggest a look here at Neo-Kantianism only where it is of interest for the development of Sesemann's thoughts. Let us start with what Cohen, Sesemann's professor in Marburg, had to say about Lipps. Cohen had a well-defined opinion about Lipps: naturally, he generally disagrees with him, because Lipps must be seen, in the first place, as advertising the virtues of an ideal "positivist aesthetic empathy" (Lipps: 369). However, Cohen nevertheless recognizes an immense advantage in Lipps's psychology precisely because, as Lipps himself declared, it is based on (or has even become) *rational philosophy*. In this sense, Cohen recognizes that Lipps's aesthetics of empathy permits a re-description of art, not just in terms of an "immediate" act of *Einfühlung*, but also in terms of its contrary: *technique*. An interesting comment by Cohen on Lipps reads as follows:

> Unsere Bedenken, die wir von vornherein gegen die von ihm angenommene *Einfühlung* angedeutet haben [...], bleiben bestehen. Aber es ist erstlich anzuerkennen, dass er es nicht bei der mythologischen Beseelung bewenden lässt, sondern in die Technik der Künste nach den Anweisungen Sempers mit umfassender Kapazität sich einzuarbeiten vermochte. Übrigens aber auch den rationellen philosophischen Standpunkt den unreifen psychologischen Einseitigkeiten gegenüber immer bewusster aufgerichtet hat (2: 203).

> Our initial doubts concerning the notion of *empathy* and the way he understood it [...] remain valid. However, we must first recognize that he does not content himself with mythological sympathy; rather he managed to become well versed in the techniques of art as conceived by Semper. Furthermore he has always made a case against immature, one-sided psychological tendencies by consciously emphasizing the rational, philosophical point of view.

The *argumentation* by which Cohen declares Lipps "tolerable" is remarkable. Cohen associates Lipps's *subjectivism* with one of the most typical brands of aesthetic *materialism* present in the humanities at that time: the aesthetics of Gottfried Semper. It is thus a combination of psychologist subjectivism and that kind of aesthetics radically reducing art to "dead material" which represents for Cohen an acceptable alternative to aesthetics in general. Cohen's motto is that "every genius has his own technique" (1: 220); and this motto he finds materialized in the philosophy of Lipps.

However, it would be premature to conclude that the aforementioned paradox disappears through Cohen's reconciliation of two extremes; on the contrary, it subsists more obstinately than ever.

B. N. O. Lossky

A critic of Lipps in Russia might, on the other hand, have encountered considerable criticism from Cohen and his school, because this critic seems, on the whole, to drift too far towards what Cohen has mocked in the above quotation as a "totale Beseelung." This critic of Lipps is Sesemann's "Russian teacher," Lossky. Opposed to all kinds of subjectivism, Lossky discovered in Lipps's philosophy a particularly vicious device, which appeared to him to be a philosophical model by means of which Lipps declares *everything* to be subjective. The disagreement with such tendencies represents one of the cornerstones of Lossky's entire "organic philosophy." If we follow Lipps, Lossky explains, then not only *objects*, but also *relationships* between objects (structures) would be subordinated to nothing more than the mind of the subject; and this is unacceptable. In his 1917 book, *The World as an Organical Whole,* Lossky writes:

> With the slightest change in point of view an object appears to us to stand in different relations, and yet this multifariousness of relations is not subjectively conditioned by the observing mind's acts of perception, as Lipps supposes it to be, but lies in the object itself (85).

It needs to be pointed out that Lossky is (together with the Formalists) among the few successful anti-positivists in Russia. At that time and earlier there were other, mostly Germanophile, philosophers in Russia who were seriously engaged in the battle against positivism but had only limited success. Most of them pursued their projects by introducing Neo-Kantian philosophy into Russia. Still, the chief representative of "Russian Neo-Kantianism" (as amorphous as this movement might be), Lossky's teacher Aleksandr Vvedensky (1856–1925), had never been able to establish a journal, let alone a school.

In general, the history of Russian Kantianism is far from glorious. Hans Kohn has described the problem of Neo-Kantianism in Russia from the point of intellectual history: "Kant's criticism and English thought found hardly any followers in early nineteenth century Russia: their cautious approach, their sense of responsibility and of limits, did not appeal to a Russian extremism which was as violent in its affirmation of faith as in its denunciation" (109).[9] Rather early Vladimir Lesevich (1837–1905) had attempted to widen the epistemological spectrum of Russian positivism by means of certain original Neo-Kantian themes. However, his reception in Russia was discouraging. Russian "extremism," political as well as religious, simply did not tend towards Kant's philosophy (109).[10] The younger group of Russian "Neo-Kantians" around *Logos* was not tightly bound to the movement and was relatively open to all kinds of philosophy, especially Hegelianism. With some irony one can say that the phenomenon contains a double bind: later, during the consolidation period of Marxism in Russia of the 1920s, Kantian philosophers were too quickly identified as metaphysicians in disguise.

There are reasons to conclude that Neo-Kantianism was traditionally difficult to establish in Russia, not simply because of an obvious lack of interest, but also, paradoxically, because any kind of re-evaluation of the metaphysical tradition would have run the risk of being received so uncritically that it would flow into the large stream of mystical idealism. The fact that Lossky's ontological intuitivism comes close to this stream, without ever entering it, makes him such an interesting figure.

However, Lossky's attack on Lipps's philosophy (which tries to establish *relationships* (structures) as purely *subjective* phenomena) brings to mind also later Russian Formalist thought. The Formalists were convinced that relationships would exist *in reality*, instead of being produced by a contemplating mind, and that they could even be modified (through certain devices) *in reality*. Lossky belonged to those who believed that Lipps's subjectivism would never be able to make us realize "the world," but that, on the contrary, it would only develop a routine kind of world view, finally giving in to all "habits of the mind." It is thus possible to detect a "Formalist lilt" in the following passage by Lossky:

> Generally speaking, our mind is so used to the impoverished world of our conventional presentations that when there is suddenly revealed to us the infinite wealth of content possessed by every object and the presence in it of an enormous number of qualities opposed to one another, we imagine that the law of contradiction has been violated. In reality, however, it simply means that we do not rightly understand that law, or have the wrong idea of the way in which the opposing qualities are combined in the object (*The World*: 128).

For Lipps, the "aesthetic form," rather than being actively produced, is but a reflection of the mind's constellations. A work of art appears to him to be a "necessary production," because we are able to locate its origin in the subjective mind of its creator. How different is Lossky's conception of art (and how much it can remind us of certain Formalist ideas): "A work of art lives outside its creator's mind with such an intensity, and bears such unexpected fruit, that he is himself amazed at his own work" (97). According to Lossky, any effect is "never wholly identical with its cause, and the reason that we distinguish it from the cause is that it does contain something creatively realized" (ibid.).

I am insisting here on the links between Formalism and earlier Russian anti-subjectivism and anti-positivism, in order to emphasize Sesemann's position as a German-Russian philosopher. Lipps's "anti-formalism," for which there is only "content" to be perceived through "aesthetic contemplation," produced different negative reactions that appear incompatible. It produced, for example, Lossky's metaphysical ontology for which "the world of harmony is a perfect creation of God, consisting of a number of beings, each of which lives in its own way in and for God" (80). At the same time it helped to produce (in the form of another negative reaction) the (Formalist) scientific conception of the world as a constellation of different (intentionally produced) structures. Lossky rejects Lipps's idea that structures are only a product of reason, and he then goes to the other extreme: the ultimate "reason" of the world does not reside in the human mind but should be sought in the world itself. It is only here, in the concrete world, that reason's "spirituality permeates the whole world, including material nature, and [...] however mysterious this may seem, the problem can only be solved by going forward into the infinite expanse of the world instead of retreating into the tiny corner of one's own self" (34).

As pantheistic as Lossky's alternative may seem, it clearly forces the mind to see *nature as a system*, even if the "organic-creative" character of this system lets the whole conception appear mysterious to an extent, as Lossky himself admits. It is certain that Lossky's conception would be far too pantheistic for Neo-Kantians like Cohen who, though he manages to exclude Lipps from his most severe criticism, still very much insists on the pantheistic character of *any* intuitionism. In an interesting passage by Cohen we find the following comment:

> Intuitive Erkenntnis nennt man, was eigentlich nicht Erkenntnis sein kann und sein soll; was kraft der Intuition die Erkenntnis übertreffen und überholen soll. Jetzt bedeutet daher die reine Anschauung nicht etwa die wissenschaftliche, die geometrische Anschauung, sondern die des reinen Denkens, welches reine Denken aber auch widerum nicht an den Ketten des wissenschaftlichen Denkens liegt, sondern dessen Reinheit in seiner Isolierung vom wissenschaftlichen Denken bestehen soll (2: 25).

> One calls intuitive knowledge that which, properly speaking, cannot and should not be knowledge; that which is supposed to cut out and

to outdo knowledge itself, by means of intuition. For this reason, by pure *Anschauung* one does not mean the scientific or the geometrical aspect, but rather the *Anschauung* of pure thinking, which will then not be bound to the chains of scientific thinking, but whose purity is supposed to consist in its isolation from scientific thinking.

The problem here is that "truth" is obviously thought of in an idealist and rather Romantic way as "absolute" (meaning abstract and removed from the real world). Speaking now about Russia, I think that one has the right to suggest (though this is somewhat polemical) that in a world which was not subtle enough to cultivate Neo-Kantian ideas, the Russian Formalists almost *had* to do what they finally did: to insist on the existence of objective structures which are supposed to hold the world together "*in reality*" (and not only "subjectively"). Ironically, one could say that the very fact that any Losskian "organicalness" was excluded from this structural network was going to cause problems later: the all-too-static nature of "real" structures required, retrospectively, the elaboration of the idea of the structure as a "dynamically animated whole."

In general we can say that this foundation of "Formalism" (be it Shklovsky's, Tynianov's or Lotman's), has never been abandoned. Neo-Kantianism also concentrated on the problem of "the dynamic" (from Cohen's elaborations of a dynamic version of the logical *Begriff* to Cassirer's reflections on the *Substanzbegriff und Funktionsbegriff*). For Formalist thought in general, dissatisfaction with the definition of an *objective* structure as necessarily *static* has been one of the most fruitful challenges for Formalism up to the writings of the modern structuralists of today.

C. The 1911 *Logos* Article and the First Formation of Sesemann's Ideas

Let us start with Sesemann's 1911 article from *Logos*, "Ratsional'noe i irratsional'noe v sisteme filosofii" ["The Rational and the Irrational in the Philosophical System"], his first publication which, though lacking originality in some points, provides interesting information about Sesemann's early development. The title certainly does sound Neo-Kantian. Around 1902 Rickert had developed, under the influence of Windelband, a thesis about the irrationality of reality. Concrete historical reality, Rickert claims, would be "irrational" in the sense that it would be infinitely complex, contingent and non-repeatable. It could not be subsumed under general concepts, i.e. a "rational," lawful, system. Around 1910, the opposition of rationality to irrationality had become, as also Gessen points out in the preceding issue of *Logos*, a commonly treated subject marking to a large extent the philosophical climate of the day (Gessen, "Mistika": 118ff.).

Rickert's influence is obvious in Sesemann's article. However, in a more specific way Sesemann tries to trace philosophical "formalism" (whose definition he does not specify here or elsewhere) back to those conceptions of rationality that, in his opinion, should be juxtaposed (on a *gnoseological* level) with the concept of irrationality. They should be confronted with irrationality: then it would finally be possible to see both rationality and irrationality as existing only through an interrelationship, somehow supporting each other.

In this article Sesemann bases his complex reflection on what he calls the "correlation between the rational and the irrational" on the observation that

> рациональным же в полном смысле слова [...] может быть признаваемо только непроблематическое, законченное в себе знание. Следовательно, поскольку для эмпирического знания эта завершенность недостижима, оно не только не осуществляет в себе высшей степени рациоланьности, но даже содержит иррациональные элементы [...] примесь, а напротив, необходимый коррелат безконечности и проблематичности об'ективного знания.

> only knowledge which is unproblematic and complete in itself [...] may be recognized as rational in the full sense of the word. As a consequence, insofar as for empirical knowledge this finality cannot be attained, not only will it not manifest a higher degree of rationality in itself, but it will even contain irrational elements [...]. These irrational elements are not a coincidental supplement [...], on the contrary, they are necessary in order to co-relate infinity and the problematical nature of objective knowledge (99).

The non-validity of the kind of "rational thinking" which constantly tries to limit itself by establishing its validity within the limits it has determined by nothing other than its own rationality, is for Sesemann one more challenge to combating positivist subjectivism. However, the scope of his anti-subjectivist examinations has now been expanded: It is directed against "naive consciousness" for which "мир явлений представляется непосредственно данным [the apparent world represents itself as *immediately given*]" (95).

It is interesting that, as if he just stepped out of a "Formalist" discussion, Sesemann relates this reflection, which is so closely linked to

Lossky's and the Neo-Kantians' criticism of the notorious philosophy of *Einfühlung*, to the necessity of seeing "форма и материаа строго соотносительны [form and material as being strongly interrelated)" (94). The knowledge of the "world of things" (мир верщей), Sesemann declares, should always be founded on a synthesis of form and matter. This means that the "objective knowledge" (opposed by Sesemann to a gnoseological idea of the "knowledge of *things*") becomes, within the discussion on the significance of rationality in thinking, a target through which he manages to demonstrate the "paradoxical-irrational character" of rationality itself.

As a medical volunteer in the Russian army during WWI

Sesemann's reflections are here lengthy, formal, and sometimes difficult to understand. But it is rewarding to follow them up to a point, be it simply because of the curious amalgam of different traditions they present. As a first step, Sesemann establishes the distinction supposed to separate formal and material elements in knowledge as a phenomenon that would, in his opinion, have an essentially relative character. The distinction between "формальные и материальные элементы знания возможно только, если положить в основу их единство, т.е. признать *относительность самого различия* [formal and material elements of knowledge, is possible only when one poses their unity as a foundation, and recognizes the *relativity of the distinction itself*]" (104). First, with regard to the entirety of discussions centered around the idea of formalism, "form" can no longer be seen as a self-sufficient phenomenon. Second, in a more general vein concerning any theory of understanding, the border always believed to exist between formal (abstract) knowledge and the "immediate" knowledge of concrete things becomes indistinguishable. Or, in other words, the contemplation of "things" now requires more sophisticated considerations.

Sesemann brings forward what has to be considered a critique of positivism: "В каждом конкретном факте заключается некоторый момент отвлечения от связей и отношений ко всей остальной действительности [In every concrete fact is contained a moment of abstraction from the links and relationships with all remaining reality]" (105). Therefore it is precisely the "method of abstraction that leads to the realization of concrete ideas" (105). Sesemann's complex examinations of the theoretical relationship between the rational and the irrational culminate in the introduction of the intellectual model of an accomplished infinity by means of which he demonstrates that through the establishment of outspokenly *rational* systems, the logical-rational and the irrational will fuse into a systematic unity. Within this unity "истинный смысл иррационального есть не что иное, как рациональность высшего порядка [the true meaning of irrationality is nothing other than a *rationality of a higher order*]" (109). Rationality appears as a phenomenon not incompatible with a philosophically elaborated notion of relativity.

What remains obvious in these considerations is the link with a problem that is as central in Sesemann's thought as it is in the Russian and German philosophers mentioned above. Rationality as it is obtained in "objective thought" becomes (like empiricism) relative as soon as we apply transcendental, idealist considerations. For Sesemann this also means that it becomes relative as soon as we force ourselves to understand objects as "things." On the other hand, positivism's over-evaluation of the subjective element necessarily leads to *another* kind of "rationalism." In the end, this rationalism will, as soon as it is confronted with a realism for which objects are "things," manifest fallacies almost identical to those of objectivism.

Interestingly, Sesemann comes close here to the ontology not only of Lossky, but also of Hartmann. For Hartmann any "materialist subjectivism" which contents itself with the "immediate absorption" of matter (believing that this would be the most *rational* thing to do) was suspect. Hartmann thought that matter is in the first place *irrational*; and any "formalism" would, as soon as it accepted dealing with dead matter, also have to accept this basically *irrational* input. In this sense, "thinking" itself, even the most *formal* thinking, could never be considered as a purely rational matter. A statement from Hartmann makes this point clear. In his essay "Diesseits von Idealismus und Realismus" ("Beyond Idealism and Realism") he writes:

> Denn Materie ist und bleibt irrational, auch wenn sie nur als Erkenntnisstoff dem Subjekt gegeben ist. Ein letzten Endes rationales Motiv ist es, das nicht in Kant allein, sondern in allen grossen

Erkenntnistheoretikern der Neuzeit die Tendenz nährt, Prinzipien seien das an sich Substratlose, Stoffreie, dasjenige, dessen Wesen in Form, Gesetz und Relation restlos aufgeht; Prinzipien sind das in sich logisch Durchsichtige, Rationale. Dem Idealismus liefert das, wenn es stimmt, einen willkommenen Rückhalt; denn das will vor allem einleuchten: wenn Prinzipien rational sind, so können sie in der Tat Sache des Denkens, des Urteils, und folglich Sache des Bewusstseins sein, während Materien und Substrate sich dem sichtlich widersetzen. Dennoch ist die Rechnung falsch... (2: 290–91).

Matter is and remains irrational, even when it is only given as a matter of knowledge to the subject. It is a rational motive which feeds not only in Kant, but also in all great theoreticians of knowledge, the view that principles would be without substrate, without matter, that their essence would be represented by form, law, and relation; principles would in themselves be logically penetrable, rational. These suppositions, if we believe them to be true, provide a backup which is especially welcomed by idealism; because one thing is particularly clear: if principles are rational, then they can truly be matter of thinking, for judgment, and, as a consequence, for consciousness. Matters and substrates, on the other hand, refuse all this. But then this calculation is wrong [...].

The question, which Kant points out as one of the most central ones for philosophy as a whole, is taken by Sesemann and Hartmann as a starting point for the development of the branch of philosophy called ontological gnoseology: how can the same objects be real and ideal at the same time? The right coordination of subjectivism and objectivism opens up reflections of an unexpected scope. Hartmann's and Sesemann's common philosophical aim turns out to be the establishment of an ontology which, as Sesemann has expressed in his review of Hartmann's *Grundzüge einer Metaphysik der Erkenntnis*, "не порождает и не построет своего предмета [...], оно лишь схватывает и постигает то, что существует до всякого познания и независимо от него [neither produces nor constructs its object [...], it only grips and grasps that which exists prior to all knowledge and independently of it]" (223). And an ontology that is supposed to perceive such a "одинаковое, и реальное, и идеальное бытые, но самому своему существу не может быть ни идеалической, ни реалистической [real and at the same time ideal being cannot, in regard to its very essence, be either idealistic or realistic]" (223).

Sesemann's conclusion in "Ratsional'noe i irratsional'noe" must be seen as immediately linked to this. The logical-rational and the irrational are distinguished only in *empirical reality*. In idealism and in transcendental thought, however, they are "едины и тождественны [unified and identical]." Since "being" itself cannot be grasped by either empiricism or idealism, the metaphysical idea of an absolute autonomy of "rationality" must also be recognized as relative. Because of the interplay of the real and the ideal, the "идея систематического единства но существу иррациональна. Принцип иррациональности перекидывает мост от эмпирических ступеней рационального к идее абсолютной рациональности [*idea of systematical unity* is essentially *irrational*. The principle of irrationality creates a bridge between empirical degrees of the rational and the idea of absolute rationality]" (1911: 109).

2. Form and "Living Rhythm": Sesemann's "Iskusstvo i kul'tura"

A. *Predmetnij, Ob'ektivnij*, Thingly

I have described the philosophical climate, as well as Sesemann's Neo-Kantian beginnings leading to his more original handling of essential questions concerning aesthetics, psychology, and ontology. In his article "Iskusstvo i kul'tura" [Art and Culture], published in 1927 in *Versty,* Sesemann produces original ideas about "structural form" that he understands as a "living rhythm," and about artistic expression as an interplay between a creative mind and its material. Sesemann regrets an "estrangement of aesthetics from concrete, living art" (185). When formulating his regrets (certainly having the pre-positivist and idealist aesthetics of Lipps in mind), he points to what appears to him to be an alternative:

> Работы г. Вельфлина у его последователей, а с другой стороны школа русских формалистов, представляют собою не только ценный вклад в теорию живописи, но имеют и чисто философское значение, указывая то направление, в котором она должна искать свой подлинный об'ект.

> The work of Wölfflin and his followers on the one hand, and the school of the Russian Formalists on the other, represent more than just a valuable contribution to the theory of painting. They have a purely philosophical significance, indicating to aesthetics the direction in which it should seek its original object (185).

In Sesemann's following elucidations of his idea of aesthetics, he continually points to the danger of "subjectivist theories" of knowledge, whose only declared aim would be to produce "objective knowledge." What would be lost through these procedures, Sesemann explains, is the "predmet."

For certain reasons I find this word difficult to translate here. Certainly, when Sesemann distinguishes between the "*predmetnyi*" and the "*ob'ektivnyi*" components of an aesthetic phenomenon he uses the Kantian terms corresponding to the Russian rendering of *gegenständlich* and *objektiv* as they generally appear in Russian translations of the *Critique of Pure Reason*.[11] However, I hesitate to take the use that the bilingual Sesemann makes here of these terms for granted and to translate, in Sesemann's discussion of the *predmetnyi* as the "most essential in aesthetic expressions," "predmetnyi" as "objective" in the sense of "gegenständlich." One reason for this is that the distinction from the *Critique of Pure Reason* looks to a large degree out of place in a discussion of aesthetics and its link to "concrete life." The second, more important reason is that such terminology has difficulty corresponding to Sesemann's article, "Beiträge zum Erkenntnisproblem I," dating from the same year, in which he explains the evil of any *Vergegenständlichung* (objectification, materialization) in philosophy and psychology.

Moreover, Vvedensky inverted the readings of these terms in his own writing, translating *gegenständlich* as *ob'ektivnyi*, and *objektiv* as *predmetnyi*. This is important not because I would hold that Sesemann intensively read Vvedensky or that he would have read much in the Russian translation of the *Critique*, but because many of the ideas Sesemann develops about *Vergegenständlichung* in these years are dramatically opposed to Vvedensky's. We cannot engage in this comparison here, but the discrepancy becomes clear when comparing both philosophers' arguments about the problem of "objectification" in dreams, for example. Formally speaking, Sesemann's use of "objectification" with regard to a theory of dreams occurs in the same way in Vvedensky. However, nothing can be more opposed to Sesemann's claim that objectification of dreams should be avoided than Vvedensky's ideas about this subject. In his *Psychology Without Any Metaphysics* (1915), Vvedensky holds "that during sleep certain representations, viz., those constituting our dreams, are objectified and thereby become dreams." Vvedensky asks: "What could be subject to objectification during sleep other than our representations?" (130).[12] This is exactly the kind of argumentation Sesemann vehemently attacks in the context of his own thoughts about dreams as an ontological phenomenon.

Since there is no English word for *predmetnyi* or *gegenständlich* other than "objective" (which erases its distinctness from *ob'ektivnyi*), I would like to render it here as "thingly." As shown, in 1911 Sesemann already talks about the "world of things" ("mir veshchei," which he translates himself into German as "Welt der Dinge"),[13] an unusual terminology for that time. In 1927, the year in which "Iskusstvo i kul'tura" was published, Heidegger's *Sein und Zeit* also appeared and was immediately reviewed by Sesemann. Therefore, Sesemann's characterization of aesthetic essence as something "predmetnyi" might indeed point more to "thingly" as opposed to "objective," than to a clearly Kantian or Russian Neo-Kantian origin. In a footnote in his *Logos* article Sesemann reflects the "thingly" against "material" (221 in the German version; this footnote is missing in the Russian version). Also these digressions on the character of the "thingly" must be considered unusual. Certainly, reflections about the Ding appear in Kant and Hegel. However, neither Kantians nor Hegelians (including the Russian ones) would construct an opposition of thing either to material or to the object. Hegel opposes the "konkrete Ding" to Kant's Ding-an-sich, but not to "Objekt." In general, both Kant and Hegel deal rather with the opposition "objective vs. subjective" ("dinglich" appears in Kant as a legal term signifying, as it still does today in German jurisprudence, "personal right").[14] Heidegger is the first to suggests the opposition of Ding to Gegenstand, insisting that the metaphysical tradition since Plato constantly neglected the former by favoring the latter.[15] It is also interesting to note that the critique of the "Objektbegriff" has not only been developed by Nietzsche and Heidegger, but also, in between, by Hermann Cohen. Cohen was aware of the semantic change of the word "object" in modern philosophy. The "object," though having passed through several stages, has never been established as something "concrete," but clung to its initial character of representation.[16]

Sesemann speaks of the "obshchaia predmetnaia osnova [common thingly basis"] of all aesthetic being. This foundation, if it exists, cannot be represented by art itself. However, it should not be looked for in an abstraction from art either. Sesemann's view on the problematic relationship between subjectivism and objectivism manifests itself through the following reflection:

> В чем же их общая предметная основа? На первый взгляд вопрос этот допускает как будто два решения: если эту основу нельзя обнаружить в самом искусстве, в его творениях, то ее следует искать вне его, а это значит: либо в самом эстетическом суб'екте (творящем или воспринимающем), либо же в тех смыслах, тех идеях, которые воплощаются в художественных образах. Оба эти пути были испробованы эстетикой, и оба они завели ее в безнадежный тупик. Ни той, ни другой концепции не

удалось нащупать предметное (обективное) единство искусства. И суб'ективно– психологическая и об'ективно–идеалистическая теория приходит мимо того, что наублее существенно для художественного творчеьбства.

What is thus their [aesthetic beings'] common thingly basis? At first glance, this question seems to allow two answers: if this basis cannot be discovered in art itself, in its works, then one has to look for it outside art. This means: either in the aesthetic subject itself (creating or perceiving), or in those meanings and ideas embodied in the artistic image. Aesthetics tried both of these paths, but they both led to a hopeless dead end. Neither one, nor the other conception managed to trace the thingly (objective) unity of art. Both the subjective-psychological and the objective-idealist theory overlooked that which is most essential in aesthetic expression... (186).

The "thingly" unity of art is neither apprehended by subjective-psychological, nor by objective-idealistic (rationalistic) conceptions of aesthetics. Both of these "false tendencies" are overcome only if aesthetics "откажется от чисто синематеческих коструكций и пригрузится прежде всего в ту предметную стихию, из которой рождается и в которой осуществляется художественное творчество в отдельных искусствах. [rejects purely systematic constructions and obtains more profound insights into the thingly element out of which artistic expression flows and in which it is realized in the different arts]" (186).

It is interesting that for Sesemann the (objectivist) suggestions of the Russian Formalists are recognized as a logical and consistent reaction to a difficult situation. However, on the grounds of their observations, Sesemann is able to reveal essential deficiencies in their thoughts. Alternatively, Sesemann points to the "structural form," which he understands differently from that of the Formalists: the "structure" must be seen as a living "rhythm" existing inside the work of art and constantly determining its nature. According to Sesemann, this is the "ближайшая задача эстетики, не подходящей к искусству извне, а руководящейся исключительно его внутренним жизненным ритмом [most intimate task of aesthetics, not approaching art from the outside but being directed exclusively by its inner rhythm]" (186).

B. "Inner Rhythm" and "Inner Form"

Sesemann points to the wholeness of the work of art, the structure of which can only be grasped from the inside. The influence of Lossky's organic philosophy (as well as the influence of Shklovsky) is evident here. However, Sesemann's "inner rhythm" is also strongly reminiscent of Potebnia's *"vnutrenniaia forma* [inner form]." Potebnia had derived this notion from Humboldt's linguistics, and it was important for Shklovsky and Bakhtin as well. Humboldt argued that a certain "inner structure" of language reflects the "spirit" of speakers. Morphology and syntax can differ with regard to this "inner form," but the "inner form" is a kind of general, formal organization still found "behind" the "individual" grammar or body of words. Potebnia developed Humboldt's thoughts[17] and there is certainly some similarity between these Humboldtian reflections and Sesemann's. Also, Sesemann does not want to restrict the "inner rhythm" to the localization of psychological quantities existing in the mind of the contemplating subject; on the other hand, he does not try to grasp the work *through* these structures as an objective, systemized, phenomenon either. Sesemann adheres to a structuralist-formal alternative in aesthetics. However, his idea of the structure itself depends firstly on Lossky's idea of the "organic whole," and secondly on Neo-Kantian ambitions to "dynamize" static, logical systems (regardless of whether these logical systems are founded on objectivism or subjectivism).

In the camp in Taishet (Irkutsk).

Sesemann's reference to "rhythm" as the true "inner form" of a work of art evokes interest beyond its association with Potebnia. The reference can also be seen as a direct derivation from the aesthetics of Cohen. Cohen also uses the idea of rhythm as an aesthetic notion capturing a "feeling" that is more than simply a subjective element, transmitted through *Einfühlung*, but that can also grasp a more objective aesthetic quality. In his *Ästhetik des reinen Gefühls* (1912) Cohen writes that "*...the life of rhythm is the life of consciousness.*

With it the feeling can go beyond the limits of man [gleitet das Gefühl über die Grenzen des Menschen hinaus]") (2: 203). Given the quality of rhythm as a transcendental power – power naturally opposed to any individualist subjectivism – it is interesting that Sesemann uses the same idea as a means of criticizing Formalism.

Despite the interesting aspects and possibilities for reflection that Sesemann's temptation to Formalist theory offers, it should not be overestimated. In the end, Sesemann's philosophical aim is not to find a *system* but a *"thing"*: a living phenomenon neither purely subjective nor purely objective. If Sesemann has ever had a close relationship with Formalism, it was certainly determined by this conviction.

C. Matter and Form

In "Iskusstvo i kul'tura," Sesemann makes a point about anti-objectivist philosophy and its relationship with Russian Formalism. He seems to concentrate in the first place on classical Formalist theoretical innovations like those by Shklovsky. Formalism's reduction of material to "dead" matter represents a reduction enabling the subjective mind to arrange matter in any way it desires. This contradicts the character of material as "things." In Sesemann's view, it also introduces a fundamentally flawed definition of the notion of structure. About the Formalist procedure of establishing "structures" he writes:

> Композиция, есть такой же формальный момент, как и все те факторы, которые обусловлены самой природой чувственного материала. Структурная форма не запечатлевается хыдожником на обрабатываемый им материал, [...] а осуществляет и выявляет лишь те эстетические возможности, [...] которые укоренены в его собственной пророде. Только на таком понятий формы и может быть построена об'ективная эстетика, как учение о предметом строе эстетического. Понятие "приема," которым пользуется школа формалистов, заменяя им понятие формы – несмотря на все свой методологические удобства – с философикой точки зрения не может считатся основопологающим. Форма, понятая только как прием художественного творчество, приобретает характер чего–то суб'ективно–произвольного и внешнего по отношению к самому материалу.

> The composition is the same formal moment as all those factors that are dependent on the very nature of the felt material. The structural form is not imprinted by the artist on the material on which he is working, [...] but the structural form materializes and reveals only those aesthetic possibilities [...] that are rooted in [the material's] own

nature. Only on the basis of such a notion of form can an objective aesthetics be created as a doctrine of the thingly structure of the aesthetic phenomenon. The notion of "device," as used by the school of the Formalists, which is for them a substitute for form – in spite of all the methodological convenience it offers – cannot be considered sound from a philosophical point of view. Form understood only as a device of artistic expression takes on a subjective-intentional character, and seems to exist without any relation to the material itself (187).

In fact, few quotations better characterize Sesemann's relationship with Formalism. As one of the first to integrate the critique of Formalism into a more comprehensive, general philosophical discourse, by pointing to Formalism's and Futurism's weakest points, Sesemann is able to predict the limited perspectives both would have in the future. This prediction, in Sesemann's eyes, would be due to more than outside factors such as political pressure. Sesemann admits that

> формалисты совершенно правы, когда настаивают на том, что, напр., поэтика должна исходить прежде всего из языковедения и что поэтому каждой главе науки о языке должна соответствовать особая глава теоретической поэтики. В самом деле в звуково составе слова, в ритме и в интонациях живой речи, в ее грамматическом и синтактическом строе, наконец, в ее семантической стороне, т.е. в ее образности, логическом смысле и эмоциональном напряжении даны все те элементы, или приемы, которыми пользуется поэтическая речь.

the Formalists are absolutely right in insisting that poetics, for example, should above all flow out of linguistics, and that for this reason every chapter of the science of language should correspond to a distinct chapter of theoretical poetics. As a matter of fact, in the sound structure of the word, in the rhythm and intonations of living speech, in its grammatical and syntactical structures, and finally in its semantic aspects (i.e. in its figurativeness, logical meaning and emotional tension) we find the formal elements, or devices, which are used by poetic language (187–88).

Sesemann's "Formalism" is an aesthetic one, and one can locate it even in those domains that are quite removed from aesthetics (e.g. psychology). A forecast of the wide spectrum which these thoughts actually have can be derived from the following remark by Sesemann:

Ведь реальность, приписываемая структурной форме, есть реальность эстетическая, которая не только не совпадает с физической или психической пеальностю, но и требует для своего простроения совершенно особой установки сознания.

Indeed the reality ascribed to the structural form is an aesthetic reality which not only has no overlap with physical or psychological reality, but which requires for its construction an absolutely distinct orientation of consciousness" (188).

This special orientation of the consciousness is based on overcoming the subjective-psychological *and* the objective-idealistic (rationalistic) elements in theory of knowledge in general. These two kinds of unacceptable abstractions, the subjectivist and the objectivist one, are, most importantly, traced back to one and the same root: to the philosophy of *Einfühlung*. Sesemann asks: "Не снимается вообще различие между чувственно–формальным и предметно–смысловим моментом в пределах самой эстетической формы? [Is the distinction between the felt-*formal* and the thingly-semantic moments not absorbed within the limits of the aesthetic form?]" (190). In the end he urges us to recognize that "в поэзии […] взаимоотношения между чувственно–феноменальным и предметно– смысловым фактами осложняются [in poetry […] the opposition between the felt-phenomenal and the thingly-semantic becomes more complicated]" (192).

This kind of anti-Formalist criticism appears to be penetrating. By philosophizing on the basis of what only a solid theory of knowledge can provide, Sesemann is among the first aestheticians (together with Croce) to recognize the non-sensical character of the Futurist notion of "заумный язык [transrational speech]." This notion, which deeply influenced European art at that time, was characteristic for the dominating cultural climate. However, Futurism, so we learn from Sesemann's elucidations, is nonsensical not in a logical, but an aesthetic way. Futurism *must* be nonsensical because it tries to "feel" the structure of artistic composition in a pure way; and this means that it tries to "feel" art as if it were "nothing." Sesemann concludes that "заумный язык, как язык, лишенный всякого предметного смысла, – есть чистая фикция [transrational speech, as language devoid of all thingly meaning, is a pure fiction]" (192). An art expressing nothing but itself does not express anything. However, any "feeling" should be the feeling of something. Structuralist empathy therefore represents a kind of objectivist subjectivism, which makes Futurism eventually run out of content.

Looking for affinities with this kind of reflections in Sesemann's contemporaries, one is reminded of – apart from Bakhtin to whom we will come in a moment – the religious philosophers Bulgakov and Florensky, who were opposing "idealist" philosophies to rationalist modernity. Bulgakov speaks of the necessity of a "natural" cultural environment that can give a "spiritual" content to formal doctrines. In his contribution article to the *Signpost* symposium he points out that "even negative doctrines, in their native land and amid the other powerful spiritual tendencies contending with them, have a psychological and historical significance which alters radically when they appear in a cultural desert and claim to be the sole foundation of Russian enlightenment and civilization" (29).[18]

Florensky, though born only two years before Sesemann, was interested in avant-garde aesthetic theory mainly in the form of the latest developments in Symbolist poetry, which also inspired his Humboldt-based linguistic theory. His symbolist ontology sees Being as created through a dynamic interchange between knower and symbolized reality, where any "abstract, colorless, impersonal 'consciousness in general'" should be replaced by a "concretely general, symbolically personal" consciousness (*Stolp i utverzhdenie,* 2: 829ff).

Sesemann shares the concern with these two authors that a rationally defined "form" will too easily run out of "cultural" content. Sesemann writes: "эстетическая форма […] обладает и своим собственным смыслом, своим собственным жизненным (а постольку и эмоциональ– ным) напряжением [aesthetic form [...] has its own meaning, its own life (and thus also emotional) tension]" (193). We can even speak, so Sesemann claims, of "смысле и связанном с ним эмоциональном напряжением [meaning and the emotional tension associated with it]" (194), meaning that authentic art cannot have an "непримиримого дуализма межды формальной и предметно–смысловой стороной [irreconcilable dualism between the formal and the thingly-semantic side]" (194).

We can conclude from this that Sesemann certainly adhered to a general spirit present in Formalist thought in as much as it represented a way to define a philosophical position opposed to positivism. However, Sesemann's notion of "aesthetic form" should be defined rather as that of a self-critical, "historically open" Formalism. In this context Sesemann is willing to evaluate the Formalist idea of form. He writes that the aesthetic form "как выразительной (независимо от ее предметного значения), способни дать современныму формализму в эстетике философское обоснование культурой [as an expression (independent of its thingly meaning) is able to provide, in the domain of aesthetics, a philosophical foundation for Formalism. Together with this we will explain the inner link between art and the rest of culture]" (195).

Quite reconcilingly, Sesemann recognizes that the Formalists might have been obliged to insist on the abstract-formal character of aesthetic expression because they had to build up a solid stand against Bolshevik materialism. When evaluating the cultural environment to which the Formalists (and he himself) were exposed, Sesemann is obviously ready to see Formalism as a counter-reaction to certain social movements:

> Они видят в ней покушение на автономность искусства, попытку подойти к художественному творчествы с совершенно чуждыми ему внехудожест– венными критериями и мерами. [...] они являются естественной реакцей против засилия тех социальных, моралистических и идеологических тенденций, которые до последнего времени господствовали в истории и теории искусств и тормозили ее нормальное внутреннее развитие. Правы формалисты и в том, что ставят в основу угла эстетики проблему художественной формы. [...] Еслы формалисты утверждают, что связь с культурой не определяет собой жизни и смысла самого искусства, они впадают в явное противоречие с фактами [...].

> They see in it an attack against the autonomy of art, an attempt to approach artistic expression with extra-artistic criteria and measures that are completely foreign to art itself. [...] They seem to be a natural reaction against the preponderance of those social, moral and ideological tendencies that have dominated the history and theory of art until recently, and "braked" their normal inner development. The Formalists are right in declaring the problem of the artistic form to be the basis of aesthetics. [...] If, on the other hand, the Formalists insist that a certain link with culture does not determine life and meaning of art itself, they will fall into a clear contradiction with facts [...] (196).

Sesemann seems thus to side with Croce when claiming that any "обращение мотива в чистый прием – первый признак ослабления творческого напряжения. [...] низводит себя на уровень пустой игры и эстетического гурманства [transformation of the motive into a pure device is the first symptom of a weakening of expressional tension. [...] It degrades into a simple play of aesthetical hedonism]" (196). It should be said in defense of the Formalists that "hedonism" was certainly one of the last things they were addicted to.[19] However, it is not only Croce who would have supported Sesemann's attempts to depict Futurism as a playful kind of hedonism. A statement almost identical with that of Sesemann, is made by a philosopher whose overall resemblance already becomes clear: Bakhtin.

Bakhtin's statement can be found in "Problema soderzhaniia, materiala, i formy v slovesnom khudozhestvennom tvorchestve [The Problem of Contents, Material, and Form in Verbal Art]" and reads as follows:

Всякое чувство, лишенное осмысливающего его предмета, ниспадает до голо–фактического психического состояния, изолированного и внекуль– турного [...] Поэтому ни к чему ни отнеценное чувство, выражаемое формой становится просто удовольствием, которое в конечном счете быть обьяснено и осмыслено только чисто гедонистически...

Any feeling, deprived of those things giving its object meaning, gets reduced to a merely factual state of the psyche, to an isolated and extra-cultural state. [...] It becomes simply pleasure that, in the final analysis, can be explained and understood only in purely hedonistic terms... (14 [trans. from 264]).

Moreover, Bakhtin's main ambition was to overcome "romantic" individualist subjectivism that he saw, perhaps by slightly simplifying things, embodied by the tradition of Herder's and Humboldt's linguistics. He saw individualist subjectivism also embodied in modern branches of psychologizing linguistic philosophy, and *at the same time* he saw it in abstract objectivism. He overcame both through a very pointed criticism of, for example, Leibniz's *grammatica universalis*, and the Geneva School's distinction of *langue* and *parole*. Finally, he saw individualist subjectivism also embodied in the Russian Formalists' opposing of content to form.

This means that, for Bakhtin and his circle, language could be neither an abstract form nor a direct "materialization" of a mysterious psychophysical energy. In this sense his thoughts overlap with Sesemann's who approached the same subjects while coming from the heart of German post-Kantian philosophy.

In a more general approach we can state that Sesemann shares with Bakhtin a quite common view on the philosophical notion that was of particular interest to Bakhtin, the notion of style, and it will be interesting to insist on this for a moment. Sesemann defines style as a quantity which has an inner link with the "zhiznennoi ustanovkoi [living world attitude]" (198) and which is thus dynamic because it is determined by real life. In this sense, for both Sesemann and Bakhtin, aesthetic form or artistic expression are neither engendered through "inner life" alone, nor do they depend on life's "objective structures;" they must be seen as a communication which an individual, creative mind entertains with the "things" that he finds in his external environment.

Sesemann asks a question that refers to a problem directly flowing out of this constellation of ideas and clearly illustrating this parallel: "не выясненным остается основой вопрос: что же собственно открыло художнику глаза на эстетическую ценность именно этих форм? [The basic question remains unclear: what was it in particular that opened the artist's eyes to the aesthetic unity of just these forms?]" (197). An interplay of subjective judgment and exterior influence, an act of *choice* that would (as it has been so often insisted upon by Lotman) subsist even within the "final" and readily determined structure. These are the only quantities which represent the ground for the creation of the aesthetic form. Finally, Voloshinov describes the same problem once again: "Индивидуальный произвол [...] никакого значения иметь не может. [...] Только то может войти в мир идеологии, оформиться и упрочиться в нем, что приобрело общественную ценность. [Individual choice [...] has no meaning. [...] *only that which has acquired social value can enter the world of ideology, take shape, and establish itself there*" (25–26/22).

These points have a broad scope in Sesemann's philosophy, but before approaching them we should look at one more example provided by a text published 10 years earlier in which Sesemann tries to reflect more radically his own thoughts as opposed to the ideas of those philosophers coming from the rather extremist front of the "Formalist" side. In an article entitled "'Lingvisticheskie spektry' g. Morozova i Platonovskii vopros [The 'Linguistic Spectrums' of Mr. Morozov and the Platonic Question][20] Sesemann deals with the kind of linguistic analysis which has the task of

> установить частоту повторяемости у разних авторов отдельных слов, в особенности служебных или распорядительных частиц человеческой речи. Метод этот, по мненю г–на Морозова, служить лучшим способом гля определения индивидуальных особенностей склада речи изучаемаго автора.

> determining the frequency of repetition of certain words in the work of different authors, especially of subordinate or extraordinary parts of human speech. This method serves best, according to Mr. Morozov, for the purpose of determining the individual idiosyncracies of the language of the examined author (1).

The work of the linguist Morozov would probably not have attracted Sesemann's interest, had Morozov not claimed that his method would, among other things, serve a particular aim: to evaluate the authenticity of ancient texts and, especially, to see if the works of Plato that are generally attributed to Plato himself as author have not been written by other authors.

First of all, the question of plagiarism or non-clarified authorship of the Platonic writings was already well known to Sesemann, as he explains:

> Изложенные в них философские учения не только расходятся между свобой, но иногда до такой степени противоречат друг другу, что нет даже возможносту считать их различными ступенями развития одной какойнибуть общей точки зрения. Неудивительно, конечно, что таком положении дел современные исследователи Платона не пришли к единогласию; и те книги, которые одними признавались подложными, другими обьявлялись подлинными – и наоборот.

> The philosophical theories present in them not only differ in different texts, but sometimes contradict one another to such an extent that it is impossible to even consider them as different levels of development of some common point of view. In such a situation it is, of course, not surprising that modern Plato researchers have not come to unanimous agreement, and that there are books which some recognize as authentic and which others declare to be falsifications, and vice versa (2).

Morozov now considers the possibility that those works were "не написаны–ли они разными авторами, – правда, – одной школы, но разных, быть может, поколений [if not written by different authors – true – of one school, but, perhaps, of different generations]" (2), which would clearly explain the contradictions in Plato's work. The "objective criteria" established by Morozov, the categories supposed to exclude the existence of a polyphony of voices within the speech of only one author, are confronted by Sesemann with a criticism based on the ground of an anti-idealist stylistic. Sesemann writes:

> При решении вопроса о подлинности произведений древности нельзя пользовать только одным критепием, а необходимо считаться со всеми существенными особенностями изучаемаго произведения. Так и критическое исследование диалогов Платона не может основиваться только на рассмотрении их идейного содержания или только на лингвистическом анализе, а

должно руководствоватся совокупностью всех приложимых к нему критериев подлинности, т.е. оно должно приимать во внимание и философское содержание, и стиль, и форму композиции, и свидетельства других писателей и пр. и пр.

When addressing the question of the authenticity of ancient works, one should not apply only one criterion; it is necessary to consider all of the essential characteristics of the examined work. Thus the critical examination of Plato's dialogues cannot be founded only on an investigation of their ideal content or only on linguistic analysis, but one has to consider the entirety of the criteria of authenticity, i.e. one has to pay attention to the philosophical content, the style, the form of composition, the testimony of other writers, etc., etc. (5).

Sesemann suggests that the web of signs represented by the text does not reflect, but *refract* reality, and that the authenticity of this reality can be sought only within this very refraction. The style of a work does not flow out of an individual, objective, *psychological* content that would express itself as a purely linguistic "self-identical" phenomenon. Instead, the style exists through its own variability within a socio-historical context. Stylistic variety is thus content-oriented, and linguistic polyphony represents a dynamic interplay also on the semantic level of Plato's philosophy. In Sesemann's view, there is nothing that could prevent us from seeing these stylistic deviations as "результаты изменения (а так же развитияъ) с одной стороны стиля Платона, с дрыгой – его философской концепции [results of the change in (and also the development of), Plato's style on the one hand, and on the other, his philosophical concepts]" (7).

Sesemann strengthens this point, interestingly, by introducing an idea that was one of his most cherished topics (and that also has a Neo-Kantian root): the idea of rhythm as an aesthetic quality. Since, as Sesemann points out, rhythm is one of the most important qualities in ancient prose in general, an interpretation of Plato's philosophy should also undergo a shift from the objective-linguistic to the "rhythmical" component of his language. More precisely, the rhythmical structure of his speech represents more than an abstract plan of his language. In fact, it provides, through its extension into social life, the grounds for ontological stylistics. Sesemann writes:

Не может быть сомнения, что изучение стиля Платона должно в первую голову заняться именно ритмической стороной вопроса, ибо только точное представление о ритмической структуре Платоновской речи создает твердую почву как для определения индивидуальных особенностей Платонова стиля, так и для лингвистического анализа.

There is no doubt that in the examination of Plato's style one must first deal with the rhythmical side of the issue, because the presentation of the rhythmical structure of Plato's language lays the foundation for the determination of individual characteristics of Plato's style, as well as for the linguistic analysis (10).

Hermann Cohen's already mentioned conception of rhythm as the "life of the consciousness" is used here as a unifying element, representing "feeling in time" (Cohen 2: 144). Apart from that, "time" as a matter for ontology is also a primary topic of many of Sesemann's later, German writings. We remember that in an already mentioned text, Cohen insists that the perception of the "formal-felt" component of the text (an expression also used by Sesemann in the context of his critique of Formalism) should not be turned into a perception of the objective-idealistic. This means that rhythm is neither pure feeling nor pure form but that it, as Cohen says, "develops beyond the human being" (ibid.).

Like Bakhtin and Croce, Sesemann is aware of both Formalism's and Anti-Formalism's tendency to turn into a non-sensical and content-lacking theory about how we should produce and understand art. However, the idea of introducing *time* into the theory of understanding, into linguistic analysis, and finally into the notion of the structure itself, seems to be rooted in Cohen's Neo-Kantian strategies. In fact, just before establishing rhythm as a timely parameter working in the service of an "aesthetics of pure feeling," it is Cohen who writes:

> Die Logik der reinen Erkenntnis hat demgemäss die *Zeit als Kategorie* ausgezeichnet. Die Zeit ist die sachliche Bedingung dass die *Unterscheidung* nicht nur ein Akt des Bewusstseins bleibt, sondern dem Bewusstsein zum Inhalt verhilft, und damit über den blossen Vorgang hinaus zu einem dauerhaften Bestande (141–42).

> The logic of pure knowledge has thus distinguished *time as a category*. Time is the factual condition that the *distinction* remains not only an act of the consciousness, but it helps the consciousness to find contents, and thereby helps it to gain the status of continuity.

In conclusion we can say that Sesemann's reflections on philosophy's obligation to consider the indispensable communication existing between form and material are elaborated on the basis of the

Formalist discussion of dynamism that was current at the time in St. Petersburg. Through this discussion, some of the rather underdeveloped parts of Formalist theory were led to fruitful self-criticism. Sesemann tried to benefit from this discussion and lets it work in the service of a more profound *Erkenntnistheorie* which attempts to transcend the narrow limits of a purely Formalist aesthetics.

Notes

1.   Sesemann contributed an article to the second issue of the periodical *Logos* (1911) that had adopted a Neo-Kantian tendency when directed by S.I. Gessen and F.A. Stepun. This article is certainly not among the most instructive ones (it was Sesemann's first publication), but it is still today quoted as a main reference on Russian Neo-Kantianism. See Thomas Nemeth's bibliography of his "Russian Neo-Kantianism."

2.   Kagan, the actual founder of the Bakhtin circle, is held responsible for the Neo-Kantian influence in the early activities of the Bakhtin Circle. Though both studied in Marburg with Hermann Cohen, Sesemann and Kagan apparently never met because Kagan had left Marburg just before Sesemann's arrival. Sesemann's friend Nicolai Hartmann met Kagan in Marburg. It needs to be said that the Bakhtin Circle partly kept a Neo-Kantian orientation through Voloshinov who began to translate Cassirer's *Philosophy of Symbolic Forms.* Bakhtin himself was under strong Neo-Kantian influence until 1929 (before his first publication appeared), but cannot really be called Neo-Kantian with regard to the rest of his work. As far as Neo-Kantianism goes, I treat Sesemann in a way that would also be appropriate for Bakhtin.

3.   "Martin Heidegger: Sein und Zeit"

4.   In general, Hartmann is said to have much in common with Scheler because of his concentration on objective, non-formal values. With Heidegger he shares a predominant interest in Being. Still it must be said that Hartmann was never interested in "Being as such" in the way in which it was taken up by Heidegger as a main philosophical theme able to provide insights into human "Existenz."

5.   The German word *Gnoseologie* is derived from the Greek word *gnôsis* (secret knowledge) and overlaps semantically with the word *Erkenntnistheorie* (see note 27). Today, the first of the two volumes of Sesemann's *Collected Works* in Lithuanian is called "Gnoseologia."

6.   See for this problem a 1927/28 essay by Max Scheler: "Idealism and Realism" in M. Scheler: *Selected Philosophical Essays.* German in *Späte Schriften.* Scheler criticizes Hartmann and compares him with Heidegger.

7.   Theodor Lipps (1851–1914), a philosopher and psychologist, developed the *Einfühlungsästhetik* [aesthetics of empathy] as a primordial occupation of psychological theory.

8.   The aging Dilthey should certainly not be excluded from discussions on psychology as it was thriving in the second half of the nineteenth century. It led to Dilthey's contribution of a "Psychologie als Erfahrungswissenschaft" ("Psychology as experimental science," title of a lecture course 1875–94). There are certainly ideas in Sesemann that are more reminiscent of those by the older Dilthey than of those by the younger Lipps. Especially Sesemann's points on self-perception might have been developed under the influence of Dilthey's notion of "self-reflection" or "reflexive awareness." In general, Dilthey's insistence on *experience* (*Erfahrung*) (that can, in some way, be opposed to the more scientific Lippsian *Einfühlung*) seems to reflect a great deal of Sesemann's strategy. In Chapter 3, I show that in the essay "Über gegenständliches und ungegenständliches Wissen" (Sesemann 1927), Sesemann consolidates his anti-subjectivist arguments by referring to Dilthey's approach of grasping an 'unmittelbare konkrete Erlebnis' (immediate concrete

experience), an approach that supposedly avoids a reduction of psychic life to abstract psychic elements and which, in Sesemann's opinion, is able to organize single elements within a living, organic whole (85). In the present chapter I concentrate more on Lipps than on Dilthey because Lipps's ideas meet with an immediate counter-reaction in Sesemann, and therefore seem to have contributed in their own manner much to the formation of his most original thoughts. One could say that Dilthey is "by nature" close to Sesemann. Any further exploration of this relationship, however, would lead us away from the path of the present exposition.

9. There has recently been interesting new literature on Russian Neo-Kantianism: West, "Art as Cognition in Russian Neo-Kantianism;" Nemeth "The Rise of Neo-Kantianism," and "From Neo-Kantianism to Logicism." See also West: "Kant, Kant, Kant."

10. *See also West who points out that "Russia's Neo-Kantians sought a formal theory of knowledge embracing both rational cognition and religious belief..." ("Art as Cognition..." 200).*

11. This goes for the first translation of the *Critics of Pure Reason* made by Mikhail Vadislavev and published in 1867 (St. Petersburg: Tiblen & Nekludov) as well as the revised edition of Lossky's early translation contained in Kant's "Works in Six Volumes" (*Sochinenija v chesti tomakh* Vol. 3: *Kritika chistovo razuma*, Moscow: Mysl', 1964).

12. *Pskhologija bez vsakoi metafiziki*. Engl. quoted from Nemeth, "From Neo-Kantianism to Logicism," note 35. See also Chapter 2. For Vvedensky's translation of *objektiv* and *gegenständlich* see T. Nemeth: "The Rise of Neo-Kantianism," note 20.

13. See the German version of the article in the parallel German issue of *Logos* 2 (1911), 208–242: "Das Rationale und das Irrationale im System der Philosophie."

14. Another possibility is also the opposition of "dinglich" vs. "sachlich." "Sache" means, in the *Critique of Pure Reason* as well as in Hegel's *Phenomenology of Spirit*, "reality." In Hegel it means also "das Wesentliche" and "das Wahre," a meaning that goes parallel with, and not in opposition to that of *Ding* (*Enzyklopädie der philosophischen Wissenschaften*, 141ff (§ 21) (Frankfurt: Suhrkamp, 1970, *Werke* Bd. 10)). An opposition of "Ding" and "Sache" existed in the 18th century in German linguistics after Wolff (cf. Johan H. Lambert: *Neues Organon, oder Gedanken über die Erforschung und Bezeichnung des Wahren und dessen Unterscheidung vom Irrtum und Schein*. Berlin: Akademie Verlag 1990 [1764]).

15. Hegel: *Enzyklopädie*, 256–257, § 125. Heidegger: "Das Ding" in *Vorträge und Aufsätze* (Pfullingen: Neske, 1985) 163–181; and *Die Frage nach dem Ding: Zu Kants Lehre von den transzendentalen Grundsätzen* (Tübingen: Niemeyer, 1987).

16. Cohen: *Logik der reinen Erkenntnis*, 68ff.

17. The notion appears only rarely in Humboldt's work and can be found in his monograph *Über die Verschiedenheit des menschlichen Sprachbaues* (section 11) and in the introduction of his main work *Kawis of Jawa* (1830–35, published after his death and translated into Russian in 1859). Humboldt's ideas, recognized only relatively late, were of importance for comparative linguistics and psycholinguistics and, on a wider scale for the work of Karl Vossler who sees the "inner form" as a kind of "subjective tendency" opposed to the "outer form" of the language received by the "listener" (see Vossler, *Geist und Kultur in the Sprache*). The Bakhtin circle was influenced by these Vosslerian ideas even before the publication of this book to the extent that Vossler's "Neo-Idealism" can be seen as the most important German doctrine present in Russia around 1910. Slightly different is the development of the Humboldtian theme by the Ukrainian philologist Alexander Potebnia (1835–1891), the main representative of Russian "psychologist linguistics." In his 1862 book *Mysl' i iazyk*, Potebnia defines "inner form" as different from "content" because "inner form" expresses the central meaning of an object pushing the perception into the direction of a *certain* content. Bakhtin's *architectonics*, as well as the Formalist notion of *composition,* are related to Humboldt as well as to Potebnia. See: E. Kotorova, 18–20; and Fizer. Also Gustav Shpet developed a notion of "structure of the word" which is not Formalist but indebted to Humboldt's concept of language as *energeia*. Around 1927 Shpet turned away from

Husserl's *Logical Investigations* and engaged in interpretations of Humboldt. It was also in 1927 that he published a book called *The Inner Form of the Word* (*Vnutrennaia forma slova: etyudy i variazii na temy Gumbol'ta*, Ivanovo: Ivanovo University Studies in Russian and Western Thought Vol. 1, 1999 [1927]).

18. The religious philosopher Sergei N. Bulgakov (1871–1944), after his Marxist phase, participated in the Signpost (*Vekhi*) Symposium (1909) that partly aimed at restoring metaphysical idealism in Russia through a pointed critique of the contemporary intelligentsia. Bulgakov adhered to this tendency of the symposium. See *Signposts – vekhi* (23). Pavel A. Florensky (1882–1937), linked, like Bulgakov, to the so-called Russian Religious Renaissance, rejected especially the rationalist side of Western religious philosophy. His main work, in which also his linguistic theory can be found developed, is *Stolp i utverzhdenie istiny,* trans.: *The Pillar and Ground of the Truth.*

19. The reproach of hedonism was also common among representatives of Lipps' *Einfühlungsästhetik* who wanted to distinguish their purely aesthetic and sublime *Einfühlung* from more common, Romantic, sensual one. More radically, Cohen would accuse *all* individuals practicing *Einfühlung* of "hedonism" (Cohen 2: 204).

20. "Mr Morozov" is apparently Petr Osipovich Morozov, born in 1854, a St. Petersburg philologist and specialist on Pushkin.

Chapter 3

New Approaches to the Psychic Subject:
Sesemann, Bakhtin and Lacan

1. Introduction

In the present chapter I want to show in which way Sesemann has linked
the question of the difference between the internal-subjective and the
external-objective in psychology to the discussion of objectivism and
subjectivism that was widespread in Germany at that time. The same
question is also central to a large part of Bakhtin's philosophy. Apart
from that, correspondences also exist between these ideas and some of the
intellectual potential that has become accessible through the work of the

psychologists and philosophers of post-
Freudian, Lacanian France.

Voloshinov (a member of the
Bakhtin circle whose relationship with
Bakhtin was such that some specialists
have agreed that his book on Freud could
have been authored by Bakhtin) criticizes
rationalistic, idealistic and psychologistic
tendencies in semiotic linguistics.
However, he equally forces us, by way of
his parallel rejection of 'individualist
psychologism', to see as pure 'fictions'
not only certain rationalistic structures that
are produced by the scientific mind, but
also any presumed 'concrete content' of a
psychological phenomenon.

At Lake Salakas (Lithuania) in 1939

Also the concrete content that we believe to exist in psychic life is no
more than an *abstraction from* psychic life. (In Voloshinov's philosophy
of language "abstractions from the life of language" are explained in a
parallel manner). Looking at one of Voloshinov's suggestions, made at
the beginning of *Freidizm*, we can note an immediate parallel between
Voloshinov and Sesemann (a connection which can also be interpreted in
the context of certain reflections on the philosophical justification of
'scientific psychology' as far as it was present in Germany at that time).
Voloshinov asks us "какой опыт должен быть положен в основу

научной психологии: внутренний – субьективный или внешний – обьективный, или может быть, какая-нибудъ определенная комбинация из данных и того и другого опыта? [which of the two kinds of apprehensions – internal-subjective or external-objective – ought to form the basis for a scientific psychology? Or might not some particular combination of the data of both serve that purpose?]"[1]

Sesemann approaches the problem of subjectivism and objectivism in psychology by concentrating on a question which has also been treated by Bakhtin and which can be formulated as follows: Even if it is possible to distinguish subjectivist and objectivist approaches through the introduction of certain methodological safeguards, one particular problem will always remain unsolved: what happens when *the subject is at the same time also the object*?

What is put into the centre of analysis here is the phenomenon of self-perception. In self-perception the *subject* (the self) is declared to be the *object* of perception as well, and is thus not only subjective but also 'objective'. Consequently, the first question to be asked is whether an 'objective self' is still able to provide *any* perception (including that of itself) because, in fact, *every* act of perception is supposed to 'go through' a subject. Sesemann defines this situation as follows:

Wie kann das Subjekt zugleich auch das Objekt sein, wenn doch für die Korrelation von Subjekt und Objekt gerade ihre prinzipielle Transzendenz notwendige Voraussetzung ist. A. Comte war der erste, der diese Schwierigkeit richtig erkannt hat; er glaubte die Möglichkeit unmittelbarer Selbstwahrnehmung leugnen zu müssen. Aber auch eine Reihe moderner Psychologen, ja vielleicht sogar die Mehrzahl derselben vertritt denselben Standpunkt [z.B. Ebbinghaus, Mayer, Janet, Lipps]. Sie erklären: Selbstbeobachtung, d.h. die Erkenntnis psychischer Erlebnisakte ist in dem Augenblick ihres Erlebens nicht möglich.

How can the subject be at the same time also the object, when the necessary precondition for the correlation of subject and object is precisely its principal transcendence? A. Comte was the first to recognize this difficulty properly; he felt himself obliged to deny the possibility of immediate self-perception. But also a range of other modern psychologists, and perhaps even the majority of them, defend the same position [for example Ebbinghaus, Mayer, Janet, Lipps]. They declare that self-observation, i.e. the recognition of psychic acts of experience is impossible at the moment at which the experience is made.[2]

Sesemann believes that a "transcendental" input is introduced into the act of perception as soon (as it is the case in self-perception) as object and subject overlap. This input must be called transcendental because in self-perception both the subjective and the objective sphere are transgressed.

Subjectivists need now to negate (since they are not willing to accept the possibility of a transcendence in the act of knowledge) not only the supporting link that normally should exist between subject and object in understanding; they also need to negate the possibility of self-perception as such. It was the German psychologist Lipps who, in taking this step, was led to the development of a special strategy. The self, so he declares, is *always* the *object* of the *past*, and, so he says, in *no* case would we ever be confronted with our own selves in the form of present things: "Ich habe also auch kein Wissen vom gegenwärtigen Ich [...], das gegenwärtige Ich ist nicht Gegenstand..." [I thus have no knowledge of the present I [...], the present I is not an object...]" (from Sesemann, ibid. 75).

By and large, the relationship between subject and object, instead of being recognized as a theoretical model from which could be derived

numerous insights into the transcendental character of "subjective psychology" in general, is "normalized" through special devices which remain, up to the present, proper to scientific psychology. It is normalized in the sense that its "circular" structure is declared to correspond to the structure of all other relationships which can exist between subject and object. We are confronted here with a case of what Sesemann calls "materialization" of subjective life. Given its persisting attempts to objectify subjective elements it is somewhat surprising that this discipline which is distinguished by an excessive methodization, still clings to its name of "subjective idealism."

With wife Wilma in 1937

In fact, while subjective idealism tries to make the subject speak to us "directly," the result of its procedure is rather the contrary: the subject does not speak at all; it has become an object, or it has become even a sign. In any case, the subject no longer has what we could call a subjective life. Münsterberg, a representative of subjective idealism, declares that "das psychologische Subjekt [...] will nichts, fühlt nichts; es findet bloss gewisse Bewusstseininhalte vor." [The psychological subject [...] does not want anything, it does not feel anything; it only finds certain contents of consciousness]."

In order to combat this kind of subjectivism Sesemann introduces, as an efficient theoretical device, the term of *Selb[sic]stellung* (presentation of the self)[3] by means of which we would be able to redefine all subjective acts of will (*Willensakte*), judgements (*Urteile*) and evaluations (*Wertungen*) as participating elements in the self-presentation of the subject. Of course, and this must be said, these *Selbstellungen* also exist for subjective idealism. Here, however, they are not accepted in the form of active creations which can be produced *by the subject* in order to be subsequently "thrown into" an analyzable mental life. On the contrary, subjective idealism feels obliged to materialize them; it needs to declare them to be "objects" which exist as, for example, "gegenständliche Bewusstseinsinhalte, (Empfindungen, Vorstellungen)" ("objective contents of consciousness (feelings, imaginations)") (82) and which are always seen as being connected to the "*Selbstellungen*" in an *unequivocal* way. We should mention here that to these "imaginations and feelings" can also be added the phenomenon of "dream," which plays an important role in the part of Sesemann's philosophy.

Sesemann's idea of the "*Selbstellung*" is, of course, very reminiscent not only of some Bakhtinian ideas, but also of Lacan's attempts to deconstruct the *cogito* in order to replace it by a more "ontological reality" which, instead of an 'I think', would rather produce an 'I am'. We can refer to a passage from Lacan's *Séminaire XI* where Lacan criticizes Descartes's methodological perception which is founded on nothing other than pure 'self-perception'. In fact, Lacan declares, all that can be perceived through this act of perception is a brilliant '*nothing*', since any 'I', as long as it exists as an abstract category, is unable to provide the 'real content' which is necessary for acts of perception in general.

Such content can be only provided by that kind of 'I' which would react not through an 'objective reason' but which would be an 'I' that is constantly confronted with the Other. In the transcript of Lacan's *Séminaire XI* we read:

> Pour Descartes, dans le *cogito* initial [...] ce que je vise le *je pense* en tant qu'il bascule dans le *je suis*, c'est un réel – mais le vrai reste tellement au-dehors qu'il faut ensuite à Descartes s'assurer, de quoi?

– sinon d'un Autre qui ne soit pas trompeur, et qui, par dessus le marché, puisse de sa seule existence garantir les bases de la vérité, lui garantir qu'il y a dans sa propre raison objective les fondements nécessaires à ce que le réel même dont il vient de s'assurer puisse trouver la dimension de la vérité.

For Descartes, in the initial *cogito*, [...] what I am aiming at as the *I think* as it swings in the *I am*, is a reality; but the true remains so far outside that Descartes must subsequently assure himself of what? – of an Other who will not be false and who, beyond this, will be able to guarantee the bases of truth through his mere existence, who will guarantee that in his own objective reason can be found the necessary foundations so that the real itself (of which he has just assured himself) can find the dimension of truth.[4]

The objectivization of subjective contents would lead to nothing more than grotesque overestimations of the validity of subjective utterances in general; apart from this, it would exclude the possibility of any willful modifications of these contents.

As the examples of Bakhtin and Lacan show, an alternative is difficult to find. Sesemann does not mention Bakhtin, and he does not seem to be aware of other anti-subjectivist arguments that had already begun to form themselves in Germany.[5] Instead, he points briefly (and in a way similar to Bakhtin) to Dilthey's approach of grasping an "unmittelbare konkrete Erlebnis" (immediate concrete experience), an approach which finally succeeds in avoiding the reduction of psychic life to abstract psychic elements and which, in Sesemann's opinion, is capable of organizing single elements within a living, organic whole (85).

In addition to this, Sesemann's exposition of a somewhat Neo-Kantian concept of intuition is assisted by the Losskian idea of "organic-ness" by which Sesemann's layout of a slightly neokantian concept of intuition is assisted. It is the introduction of self-reflexivity, which does not appear in the form of a purely abstract act of perception, which helps to define "intuition" as a procedure, which is able to represent an alternative to the approaches of scientific psychology.

We should try to make this point clearer. "Immediate intuition" is, as Sesemann would say, not impossible as such, but is always inscribed into an interplay between the feeling subject and itself, i.e. between subjective feeling and the consciousness which the subject has of itself *as a feeling subject*. Sesemann concentrates on this fact which is as subtle as it is decisive:

Die Identität des Kenntnisnehmenden und Fühlenden oder überhaupt Erlebenden ich ist nur dadurch fassbar, d.h. ich, der Kenntnisnehmende kann das Fühlen eben als mein eigenes Erlebnis nur dadurch erkennen, dass ich bereits im unmittelbaren Erleben meiner als Fühlender, Erlebender inne werde, dass also die Erkenntnis meines Erlebens nicht als ein Anderes und Neues zu dem Erlebten gleichsam von Aussen herantritt, sondern unmittelbar aus seiner ursprünglichen Bewusstheit oder genauer Selbstbewusstheit hervorwächst.

It is only the identity of the perceiving, feeling person or the experiencing I in general can be apprehended; this means, I, the perceiving person can recognize the feeling as my own *Erlebnis* only in that I become conscious of myself as an experiencing person already within the immediate experiencing of myself as a feeling person; this means that the knowledge of my experience is not added, so to speak, from the outside, as an Other or a New to what has been experienced; but it is immediately growing out of its original consciousness or self-consciousness (95).

If this self-reflexive aspect (in which all manifestations of psychic appearances are involved) is not sufficiently considered, then psychic experiences will become "objective." This means that they will be derived from a purely subjective intuition which will no longer provide a perspective of multi-layered psychic "things" (wills, judgments, evaluations) but only on "appearances" (sentiments, imaginations). In the end, these appearances even run the risk of being considered as representing "shadows" of the life of physiology.

In general Sesemann's philosophy is marked by an ambition to establish a non-subjective aesthetics. For this reason, any "intuitionism" is seen as reductive and is explained by deriving arguments from anti-subjectivist theories in psychology. Not only does "*Einfühlung*," as it was held by Cohen, always ask for an "*Eindenkung*." By this contemplative aspect (which should be enclosed in every act of *Einfühlung*) understanding is referred to its decisive inner moment of self-reflexivity. In other words: *Einfühlung* demands contemplation; and contemplation is also always self-contemplation.

By drawing on this model, Sesemann manages to liken the formalism of scientific psychology to the formalism of the Russian formalists. Though they are, generally speaking, essentially different, Sesemann shows that both procedures are bound to produce the same result.

The Russian Formalists declare "form" (or the device) to be something completely subjective-intentional; nothing exists "inside this form" which could not be traced back to a formal, "willful" capacity of arranging the world within certain (abstract) constellations. As a consequence, for the Formalists, reality appears as a constellation which *already* forms certain structures (and which makes sense only in this manner). The formalist theorists as well as formalist (futurist) artists, will then re-describe the world in the form of what one could call a "stylized shadow play of reality." In other words, the world can be represented as an artistic reality consisting of a world with "laid bare structures."

The parallel with intuitivism becomes obvious here through the introduction of a special perspective: intuitivism (and its inheritors, the scientific psychologists) see reality as being perceived by a neutral 'I' which can perceive no more than "reflexes" of the world, by denying the possibility of any *Selbstellung*. Accordingly, Sesemann's final account established for intuitivism represents a basis for the *rapprochement* of formalism and scientific psychology.

> Das Entscheidende und Grundlegende [in der Wahrnehmung] ist die Verschiedenheit der Bewusstseinseinstellung und dem entsprechend auch der Gegebenheitsweise. Gerade dieses entscheidende Moment wird aber durch den Terminus Intuition verwischt.

> What is decisive and fundamental [in perception] is the difference in attitude of consciousness and, correspondingly, in the ways in which things are given. And it is precisely this decisive moment which is blurred by the term intuition (125).

Sesemann's observations concerning the philosophical objectivization of reality that *runs in parallel* to the objectivization of psychic life, can be spectacular. For example, when analyzing, in a text entitled "Das Logisch-Rationale,"[6] Humeian empiricism and its pretension to objectivity, Sesemann criticizes Humianism by pointing to essential equivalences which exist between Humeian and formalist thought. Through this procedure the parallelism between a "philosophy of intuition" and a "philosophy of form" becomes rather obvious.

While the formalists were trying intentionally and intellectually to transgress all habits of the mind in order to apprehend reality, the "habits of the mind" in Hume's empiricism, become the only formal criterion on whose ground the perception of reality is declared to be possible. However, the radical subjectivism and psychologism which is inherent in

Hume's philosophy, according to Sesemann, are only possible through an equally radical *objectivization* of all psychic phenomena (and from there comes the parallel with the formalists).

This time it is not the 'feelings' or the 'imaginations' (as in modern psychology) which represent the objective psychic elements; in Humeianism they are represented by a phenomenon which was already the central for German anti-positivist critics: impressions. Impressionism, this most positivist of all aesthetics, is unable to grasp the reality of psychic life, for the reason that psychic life itself is (self-reflectively) dynamic and irreducible to static impressions of the mind. Accordingly, Sesemann writes about Humeian empiricism:

> Die Objektivität der Dingwelt und ihre gesetzmässige Ordnung wird auf Gewohnheiten des Bewusstseins zurückgeführt. Trotz dieser Wendung ins Subjektive und Psychologische bleibt die Grundeinstellung der Humeschen Erkenntnistheorie dennoch eine gegenständliche. Die Struktur der Bewusstseinswelt erscheint als ein Analogon der Dingwelt. Sie ist atomistisch. Ihre letzten Elemente, die *Impressionen*, sind *statische*, relativ konstante Gebilde...

> The objectivity of the world of things and its lawful order are attributed to habits of the mind. In spite of this tendency towards the subjective and psychological, the basic disposition of the Humeian theory of knowledge remains an objective one. The structure of the world of consciousness appears as an analogue to the world of things. It is atomistic. Its last elements, the *impressions*, are *static*, relatively constant configurations (149–50).

In Sesemann is manifest, whilst he is struggling with modern psychology, a clearly Losskian ambition to discover the *real world* also in *psychic life*, the *real world* with all its wealth and colorfulness, instead of contenting oneself with impressions that are determined by abstract psychic structures. However, it is his strong awareness of the parallelism which exists in regard to objectivizations between the 'thingly' *and* the psychic world which forbids him to sympathize with materialism, and this distinguishes him from Cohen. Real matter is not consciousness, this is clear, however, it is not dead 'matter' either because, if it were, it would be too easy to lead it, in the form of impressions, to an objectified consciousness. The conclusion is that neither real life nor psychic life is consciousness. Consciousness itself arises only through a contact between both, and this contact is produced within an "unmittelbare Erscheinung" (immediate appearance). Sesemann's definition of "contemplative intuitivism" reads:

> Das materiale Sein, ebenso wie das organische (das Leben), ist in seiner unmittelbaren Erscheinung nichts weniger als bewusst-sein oder Denken. Und das gleiche gilt auch vom psychischen Sein, wenn man es nicht von vornherein unrechtmässig mit gegenständlichem Bewusstsein identifiziert.

> Material being as well as organic being (life) is, in its immediate appearance, nothing less than being-conscious or thinking. And the same is true for psychic being when one does not identify it from the beginning and in a wrong way with consciousness (184).[7]

The preceding quotation is not only a concentrated summation of the main concepts which Sesemann acquired from Lossky and the Russian Formalists; it also shows one his central ideas in regard to objectification in general: experienced Being (the psychic and the real one) can be all too easily objectified through an equation of itself with consciousness or simply with thinking (the same is true, of course, for the unconsciousness).[8] However, experience, as Sesemann claims, signifies acting and *responding to* real life; and Being exists only (similar to Bakhtin and Lacan) as a response of the I to the other. Experience exists as a production which flows out of the contact with other Beings.

2. The Logic of Being

Being does not exist within the realm of logic and not even within the realm of thinking. On the contrary, the creation of *logic* as a formal discipline *flows out of* the consideration of Being. Consequently, in an essay which takes up logic as a subject of examination, Being is determined as a quality which is not dependent on subjective conditions, but which obviously goes through a process of subjectivist elaborations as soon as it appears as a subject for knowledge; and 'logic' enters into the process of understanding only on *this* level. It does not constitute the structure of Being itself. Sesemann writes about this special relationship between Being and thinking: "In keinem Fall sind die logischen Gesetze ursprünglich und wesenhaft Seinsgesetze, sondern kommen dem Sein erst zu, sofern es den Forderungen der Erkenntnis unterstellt, d.h. der Ordnung und den Gesetzen derselben gemäss verarbeitet wird." [In no case are the laws of logic originally and essentially laws of Being, but they pertain to Being only as far as it is submitted to the requirements of knowledge; this means only when it is elaborated according to the order and the laws of knowledge]" (183–84).

Sesemann's conception of Being which bears, through a dialectical relationship between subjective and objective thinking, a hermeneutic potential, is linked to an idea of *knowledge* as a process which contains a moment of *construction*. This means that Being is not yet known at the beginning, but it is to be *constructed through* knowledge. In this way, the process of knowledge is, instead of being founded on logical laws that would be inherent in Being itself, 'only' determined by the desire to pass from non-knowledge to knowledge. What is needed is a tension residing within the logical paradox to which knowledge is submitted, and which serves, every time one wants to push knowledge towards a 'higher' form of the understanding (of Being), as a producer of that kind of energy. Positive, logical laws, on the other hand, which would exist *in Being* could not function as a producer of such an energy.

This is made particularly clear by Sesemann in an article which deals exclusively with the problem of logical paradoxes, and which seems to make of the aforementioned old Platonic paradox of knowledge (on which is founded an entire hermeneutic tradition) the focal point of all there is to say about the relationship between knowledge and logic. Sesemann speaks of the

> …schon seit Sokrates und Plato bekannte paradoxe Sachlage, dass das Problembewusstsein, in dem das Sein als noch unbekanntes vorgegeben ist, das Wissen des Nichtwissens, das Fundament für die Beurteilung und Bewertung der positiven Leistungen der Erkenntnis bildet. Ihr Schwerpunkt liegt ausserhalb ihrer selbst. Sie wird, indem sie über sich hinausdrängt.

> …paradox already known since Socrates and Plato, that the consciousness of the problem in which Being is still presented as something unknown, forms the knowledge of the non-knowledge, forms the foundation for the judgment and evaluation of the positive achievements of knowledge. Its essential point resides outside itself. It comes into being only by transgressing itself.[9]

(Historical) empiricism which gathers 'Being' in the form of facts is not 'formalized' through a retrospective application of (non-historical), abstract, logical laws. Being can never be grasped like this and this is so for the same reason for which structuralist (or Russian formalist) procedures have been declared to be contentless and purely formal. Only the consideration of *matter* as a not yet objectivized quality which determines the process of knowledge (and even its formal structure) is able to bring about a dynamical knowledge of 'non-objectivized' things. In fact, we can state that the formalist subject of 'dynamics' is treated here on the rather sophisticated level of an *Erkenntnistheorie*. According to Sesemann we should recognize that the

> …Form oder Struktur des Naturgeschehens [...] nicht der Quantität und Verteilung des Realen als ein unabhängiges starres System von Gesetzen gegenüber[steht], sondern mit [...] der "Materie" des Realen innerlich verwachsen und insofern auch mehr oder weniger veränderungsfähig [ist].

> ...form or structure of the natural event [...] is not opposed, as an independent and rigid system of laws, to the quantity and distribution of the real, but [it is] intimately and organically fused with the "matter" of the real and in this way it is also, more or less, capable of changing (77).

3. Being as Dream: Between Sleep and Waking

It is particularly interesting that Sesemann links the problems of human knowledge to the foundation of psychology. For Sesemann, Being is not logical as such because it is not necessarily a matter of thinking or of consciousness; it can only *become* a matter of consciousness by becoming a subject for human knowledge. Having said this, Sesemann points to the fact that what is true for the consciousness as a non-objective quality, is, of course, also (or even more) true for the unconscious.

In scientific psychology the objectifying consciousness is (necessarily) equated with a "gegenständliche Wachbewusstsein" [objective consciousness of the state of wakefulness]" (55); and through this device the unconscious can – paradoxically – easily be relegated to the subjective sphere of sleep. However, what remains excluded from this conception is the very dynamism which exists (since Plato) not only within the production of knowledge, but also within the production of any consciousness of the world; and it is this dynamism which also makes relative the relationship between the states of sleep and waking.

The part of Sesemann's philosophy in which these questions are treated offers an immensely rich elaboration of the status of the conscious and the unconscious as states of mind, an elaboration which lets the *erkenntnistheoretische* foundation that has been provided in the texts that we have been treating previously appear extremely relevant for contemporary philosophical questions. Being is, as has been said, not a matter of logic, and therefore the perception of Being as we encounter it through our consciousness is not at all determined by logical laws that would be provided by Being itself; and this has decisive consequences not only for the "logic of the consciousness," but also for that kind of "logic" which governs the domain of the unconscious.

The images which exist in our memory or the images which appear in our dreams are all too easily 'objectified' by giving them the status of the aforementioned imaginations or by considering them simply as a 'content' that can be contained safely in our consciousness; they are also objectified by being called *impressions* which exist in our sub-consciousness in the same way in which they would exist in our consciousness. First of all, it is clear that for this kind of philosophy the images of dream turn out to be 'less impressive' than those of reality. As a consequence, the fact of being 'less impressive' is easily seen as the *only* characteristic which makes 'real images' different from the images of the dream. Apart from this, the objective (though unclear) impressions which are represented by the images of our imagination can as easily be inserted into a logical structure that would be granted by the Being of reality. In fact, such an 'impressionist' conception of dream is even able to found an entire 'aesthetics of dreams' on nothing other than a dream's lack of impressive power. Such an aesthetics can borrow from Hume's 'subjective empiricism', which declares psychic phenomena to be neutral impressions which come 'from the outside' and which have been arranged according to subjective laws; and it can also borrow from positivist 'impressionist' formalism.

In opposition, Sesemann tries to establish 'subjective life' as a matter of logic, saying that we should recognize a special kind of logic as being particular *to subjective phenomena only*; and this kind of logic is incompatible with the logic of 'objective life'. In other words, a logic of dream can never be reduced to the kind of formal logic that does nothing

other than establish a certain abstract structure within dreams. This means: Dream is not unclear because the objective images that are contained in dream would reach the human mind in an 'improper' way. On the contrary, dream is unclear and "*unbestimmt*" because its structure follows a logic of its own. The elements which appear in a dream are not simply "unordered" and do not appear as non-logical in regard to that kind of logic

In 1957, after his release from the camp

that would be inherent in the Being that is encountered in non-dream. On the contrary, the logic of dream *is a logic*, and this is finally the main characteristic through which the Being of dream receives its dreamlike quality. In this way, the distortions or "false" ("illogical") identifications which appear in dream never appear as deficiencies that have been introduced only *"zufällig"* (accidentally); on the contrary, they are *necessary* for the composition of the structure of dreams. Sesemann expresses it like this:

> Das "So" ist auch ein "Anders" und setzt diesem Anders als Seiendes keinen Widerstand entgegen. Es kann daher ein Anders werden, ohne sich eigentlich zu wandeln und zu verändern. – Gewiss macht sich hier vielfach auch eine gewisse Undeutlichkeit, Unvollständigkeit oder Verworrenheit geltend, welche ihr Ineinanderfliessen und Verschmelzen erleichtert; aber eben nur erleichtert, nicht jedoch hervorruft. Denn es handelt sich hier nicht um die blosse Möglichkeit eines So- oder Andersseins (wie in der verworrenen Vorstellung), sondern um eine schlichte Realisierung des So und Anders in Ein- und Demselben. [...] Darin besteht aber gerade das Eigentümliche solcher Traumbilder, dass die logische Unstimmigkeit hier zur Tatsache wird, ohne jedoch als nonsense, als Absurdität empfunden zu werden.

> The "Like this" is also a "Not-like-this" and, as a Being, offers no resistance to the "Not-like-this." It can thus become a "Not-like-this" without really changing or transforming. – Certainly, there is also a certain unclearness and a non-completeness or confusion which fosters their "confluence" and fusion; but it only fosters it, it is not its cause. Because we have here not just the mere possibility of "being like this" or "being differently" (like in a confused representation); but we have a simple materialization of the "being like this" and at the same time "not-like-this" within one and the same thing. [...] And the particularity of dream images means that this logical erroneousness simply becomes a fact without turning into nonsense and without appearing as an absurdity.[10]

The world of dream as a world which exists in the domain of the psychic has obviously lost its status of 'subjectiveness'. For the materialist psychologists, this kind of subjectiveness represented the main reason why elements of psychic life could never be inserted into the system of an objective logic. Subjective elements were considered to be too 'unclear' to function in an effective way within such a structure.

Furthermore, for Sesemann the images of a dream, as well as all kinds of perceptions, imaginations, moods and feelings, cannot be seen as objects of knowledge. However, we should see these phenomena as *Seinsphänomene*; and this also means that we should see them as following a logic of their own: from a certain point of view, they are *logically irrational*. In any case one must refrain from thinking that the fact that these Beings appear as 'less clear' and 'foggy' would weaken their experiential quality *as Being*. On the contrary, their unclearness represents a *part of their Being*; and it would be wrong to simply trace this Being back to a consciousness which only works in a less efficient way. In this way, too, the lack of 'im-pressiveness' does not necessarily imply (as naive intuitionalists were bound to think) the faint coloring of its ex-pressions. On the contrary, lack of clearness in the (for example artistic) expression can be due to 'formal' (logical) distortions of the object as well as to other forms of lack of clarity; in no way is it necessarily due to a lack of 'life' within the impression.

In other words, 'imaginations' and feelings and, (if we direct our intention in the direction of clinical psychology), the manifestations of the *Trieb*, as far as it represents the subject of scientific psychological interpretations of dreams, are not unclear; on the contrary, it is the *experience itself* through which these images (of dream or of art) have been obtained which *was unclear* and which led to a perception of 'unclear' phenomena. It is thus generally erroneous to explain incompleteness or indeterminedness in psychic Being as a deficiency of consciousness which would, in a way, prevent us from perceiving the subjective contents of mind as an (objective) Being. Subjective Being, with all its indeterminateness and incompleteness, represents a Being in itself; and its 'objectivization' through the conscious mind, which tries to fill in the gaps that it believes to be missing in the dream or in the imagination, represents a completely false procedure.

At this point of our examination we should emphasize that Sesemann's insights into an 'ontology of dream' are to be seen as quite unique in the Eastern and Western Europe of his time. It is true that Freud was, especially in the Soviet Union, a subject of criticism, and the renunciation of 'spiritualist' tendencies that one observed in Freudianism, tendencies which would, one thought, all too easily exclude the *social* existence of man, did open up at least a part of their horizon in the right direction. However, with the exception of the Bakhtin circle, these approaches have almost never been developed in a consistent way but rather ended up as evocations of a remarkable number of variations of Pavlovianism.[11]

Thus Sesemann's elaborations of dream as an 'anti-subjectivist' phenomenon, are positively in advance of their time. In fact, it is Lacan who, forty years later, would describe the experience of a dream from the point of view of the dreamer in a rather similar way:

> Il vient tellement en avant, avec les caractéristiques en quoi il se coordonne – à savoir l'absence d'horizon, la fermeture, ce qui est contemplé dans l'état de veille, et, aussi bien, le caractère d'émergence, de contraste, de tache, de ses images, l'intensification de leurs couleurs – que notre position dans le rêve est, en fin de compte, d'être foncièrement celui qui ne voit pas. Le sujet ne voit pas où ça mène, il suit, il peut même à l'occasion se détacher, se dire que c'est un rêve, mais il ne saurait en aucun cas se saisir dans le rêve à la façon dont, dans le *cogito* cartésien, il se saisit comme pensée. Il peut se dire – *Ce n'est qu'un rêve*. Mais il ne se saisit pas comme celui qui se dit – *Malgré tout, je suis conscience de ce rêve*.

> [The dreamer] is so far ahead in using those characteristics to coordinate himself (absence of a horizon, closure – which are contemplated when awake – as well as the qualities of emergence, contrast, and marking of its images, the intensification of their colors) that our position in dream is, ultimately, basically that of a person who cannot see. The subject does not see where it leads him, he follows; in order to detach himself, he can even say that this is a dream; but in no case will he be able to grasp himself as such in the dream in the same way in which, in the Cartesian *cogito*, he grasps himself as a thought. He can say to himself: *it's only a dream*. But he does not grasp himself as the one who says to himself: In spite of everything, I am consciousness of this dream (*op. cit.*, 72).

It is certainly not too biased to say that Sesemann has transferred a part of Lossky's ontological intuitionism to the level of a discourse which is directly derived from the problematics of modern psychoanalysis. In fact, Lossky was certain that the *logic* by means of which the 'conventional' world is perceived by our everyday mind provides – since this mind is obviously so well trained in perceiving only the world's 'conventional' presentations – only impoverished images of the world. But, as Lossky said, this logic can be transgressed as soon as we decide that the perception of the world is no longer dependent on the habits of our mind. What we are doing then is discovering the world in terms of what seems to be illogical; and we also see, as Lossky put it, the "contradictory qualities" within the infinite wealth of content that is possessed by every object. These logically contradictory qualities should not be rejected because they do not match the logic of our subjective mind. On the contrary, so Lossky explains, "it simply means that we do not rightly understand that law, or have a wrong idea of the way in which the opposing qualities are combined in the object" (128).

4. A Timely Ontology of Dream

In the light of our previous consideration of the non-subjective character of dream we are now in a position to see *time* as a phenomenon which normally dictates a certain 'logical' order within human perception by dividing up the world which is perceived into past, present and future. Primarily, time seems to be founded on a logical necessity that is provided by real life as well as by its perception. The question which attracted Sesemann's interest so much (and which was also essential to Lossky) is whether time, by which the Being of reality is granted a logical structure, does not also represent the ground for an interpretation of mental life. Lossky especially found it necessary to insist that "mental life, which takes place in time, requires a connecting principle in order to form a systematic whole in which the past and the future could subsist in relation to each other." However, he also insisted, "such a principle must be super-temporal, for otherwise it could not simultaneously determine that which refers to *different* moments of time."[12]

Lossky's reflection projects us into the very question which was most central for Sesemann. We have already recognized both Lossky's and Sesemann's aim of the creation of a psychology which refrains from the 'objectification' of subjective, mental life; we now see that both philosophers were carrying out their project by evaluating the status of *time* in perception.

If subjective life consists of 'memories' or dreams (which all contain a particular amount of subjective will, personal evaluations, etc., and which we should avoid objectifying), it is very essential to respect the 'timely logic' of subjective events; in other words, it is important not to transfer dreams or memorized events to the level of *presence* in order to transform them into *objects* of examination for our research. For this reason, the relationship between present and past needs to be re-thought in general. Put into the most simple terms one can say that the past cannot be 'made present', either by means of memorization or by means of more sophisticated scientific considerations. And a 'subjective being' that has been manifest in the past (in the form of dreams, for example) should be recognized as a phenomenon which resides in its own sphere and which has (as Sesemann expressed it) its own *Seinsweise*. Neither the most spontaneous form of apprehensions of the past ('memorization') nor the most sophisticated *einfühlende* methods will be able to make past things *present*.

However, we should first have a look at Lossky who writes, in a similar way, along these lines:

> The validity of science can only be vindicated by the aid of an immanent theory of memory – a theory, i.e. according to which the past, in and through the act of remembering, becomes once more immanent in the subject's consciousness. The past does not thereby become present: the only thing that is present is the act of consciousness directed upon the past (43).

The same is true of attempt to ascribe present psychic manifestations to a kind of life which obviously existed in the past but which is no longer accessible as a present event: this project is also a part of the general program to objectivize subjective life. However, we should recognize that psychic life does always contain its own presence, a presence which is formed by a network of other psychic events, regardless of whether these events are conscious or unconscious. Whenever we try to see psychic phenomena as Beings that cannot be explained on the basis of their own presence but which are due to a more obvious, "objective" past, we will be led to that kind of materialism which aims to link psychic phenomena to physiological facts. Sesemann writes:

> Will man im Unbewussten nicht bloss physiologische Vorgänge und Dispositionen sehen (wie es die materialistische Deutung tut), sondern es als besondere Seinsweise des Psychischen anerkennen, so lässt es sich offenbar nur aus der Einheit des Psychischen heraus fassen, d.h. aus seinem Zusammenhang mit denjenigen psychischen Phänomenen, die unmittelbar gegenwärtig sind, und das sind die Phänomene des Bewusst-psychischen.

> If one wants to see in the unconscious not only physiological events and constellations (as it is done by materialistic interpretation), and if one recognizes it as a special way in which the psychic has its Being, then one can apprehend it only out of the unity of the psychic, this means out of its context with those psychic phenomena which are immediately present, and these are

the phenomena of the conscious-psychic. (*Die logischen Gesetze und das Sein*: 108)

Sesemann's theory of psychic Being contains an anti-Freudianism which pronounces itself against the separation of conscious and unconscious elements and which is against all theorizations of the unconscious as long as 'theorization' means no more than the 'objectification' of the unconscious in the sense that its expressions should be made as 'objective' as those of the consciousness.[13]

Though Sesemann's early criticism of psychoanalysis is remarkable in the context of the entirety of existing international reactions on Freud, it can be considered yet more remarkable that Sesemann has managed to link his criticism to the development of a special philosophical conception of time, a conception which appears as being very well anchored in the overall construction of a large philosophical work.

In general, Sesemann's philosophy of time has gone through many elaborations. However, its principal aim has always remained to link time to Being, an idea which places Sesemann in proximity of Heideggerian procedures. Sesemann's idea of logic which we have already examined as a formal phenomenon rooted in time, may be considered from the point of view of Being as an existential quality. In this way it is notable that Sesemann's book *Die logischen Gesetze und das Sein* treats, as Hartmann observed in reviewing it, "weit mehr vom Sein als von den 'logischen Gesetzen'" ("much more of' Being' than of 'logical laws'").[14] And also Sesemann himself points out in his review of Heidegger's *Being and Time,* that *Being and Time* would be "самая замечательная из всех, которые вышли за посление 10–15 лет по оригинальности и глубине; с ней могут быть сопоставлены лишь самые лучшие произведения М. Шелера" [the most remarkable [book] to come out in the last ten or fifteen years; in originality and depth it can only be compared to the best works of M. Scheler][15] In fact, in regard to the objectification of Being, Sesemann finds that Heidegger

совершенно прав, указывая на то, что, со времени античности вплоть до последнего времени, несмотря на неустанную борьбу философской мысли против овеществления нематериального, духовного бытие, бытия тем не менее по существу понималось только, как бедное, наличное бытие, а потому и категории определяющие это последнее, рассматривались как структурные начала всякого бытия. От этаго античного предрассудка не освободились окончательно ни Кант, ни представители после–кантовского идеализма.

...is certainly right in showing that from the time of antiquity, up to the most recent times, in spite of the infatigable fight of philosophical thought against the objectification of an immaterial, spiritual Being, Being was essentially understood as only a poor, really available Being, and therefore also the categories by which it is determined were thought of as structural principles for all being. Neither Kant nor the representatives of post-Kantian idealism freed us from this ancient prejudice (122).

It is interesting to see how Sesemann's theoretical elaborations of the notion of psychic Being lead him to the definition of Being in general; this definition of Being comes, as he points out himself, close to that of Heidegger. However, before coming to Heidegger, we should refer to one of Sesemann's basic thoughts, a thought which shows in a very clear way which relationship it is that Sesemann believes to exist between Being and time.

Zenon's logical paradox of the arrow which *moves* whilst flying, though it is at the same time *motionless* within each of the points that it is passing through shows that Being as a dynamic notion needs to be confronted with the phenomenon of time. Sesemann writes:

Der fliegendePfeil ruht. Denn: um vom Punkte A zum Punkte B zu gelangen, muss der Pfeil vorher in allen Punkten, die zwischen A und B liegen, gewesen sein. Das 'Sein' in diesem Punkte bedeutet aber 'in diesem Punkte unbeweglich sein', in ihm ruhen, da jede Bewegung von einem Punkte zu einem anderen fortführt und das 'Sein' in einem Punkt notwendig ausschliesst.

The flying arrow is in a state of repose. Because, in order to get from point A to point B, the arrow must have earlier passed all the points which exist between A and B. But 'Being' within this point means 'to be not in movement at this point', reposing in it, because every movement leads from one point to the other and does necessarily exclude the 'Being' in one point (*Die logischen Gesetze*, 123).

The logical irrationality contained in the timeliness of the movement can be covered but not neutralized by these interpretations provided by physical science. However, like Heidegger, Sesemann does not recognize the usefulness of a physical, *abstract* concept of time. The concept of time of physics is abstract in the sense that it declares time to be objective as something which is always *past* and thus divisible into single, distinct moments. This is the idea of time prevalent in the history of Western philosophy.

Even Hegelian dialectics remains within a logical-abstract sphere within which it will always be unable to grasp a concrete becoming of Being. Intuitionism, on the other hand, believes in being able to grasp Being, but, since it refers to the very essence of its intuition as to something which reaches, by principle, beyond philosophical conceptualization, its act of intuition becomes empty and formal, by relying on a method which itself is too far removed from the concrete world.[16]

A strong dissatisfaction with all those philosophical concepts which make of Being an abstract quality only because one is unable to cope with Being's timely aspect is present not only in Heidegger but also in Nicolai Hartmann, and we should briefly examine one of his elaborations on this very phenomenon. In an article called "Zeitlichkeit und Substanzialität" Hartmann describes how consistently, in the history of philosophy, metaphysical speculation has neglected the *substance* of the life of the real world by concealing it under its abstracting systematizations. Hartmann writes:

> Die Geschichte der Metaphysik ist eine ununterbrochene Kette von Versuchen, das Unvergängliche [...] zu finden. Der Radikalismus dieser Tendenz spricht sich deutlich in den Fassungen solcher spekulativen Begriffe aus wie 'das Absolute', 'das Unbedingte', 'das Unendliche'. Man rückte aber die Substanz nur ins Zeitlose hinaus; und man merkte nicht, dass man sie eben damit preisgab.

> The history of metaphysics is a permanent chain of attempts to find [...] the permanent. The radicalism of this tendency becomes manifest in the invention of spectacular concepts like 'the absolute', 'the unconditional', 'the infinite'. But all this did was to displace the substance into the non-temporal; and one did not notice that one was annulling it in this way.[17]

Obviously, Sesemann is concerned by the same problem and, as an alternative, he devises a notion of Being which is highly reminiscent of that of Hartmann: a Being which is not just real but only '*possible*'. It should be pointed out that Sesemann, in expounding these reflections, comes close to philosophical treatments of structural phenomena, which makes of him, once again, a negotiator between the formalists and the German tradition.

From the paradoxical character of movement in time one can derive an equally paradoxical character of Being. If we consider what Sesemann has laid down about psychic Being, that it should not be made present by inserting it into the necessary structure of 'objectified Being', we can also understand that Being in general exists only through its possibilities. Being (though this might be more obvious for psychic Being and for dream than for 'real' Being) is founded on the *ontological* existence of its possibilities. By 'ontological' Sesemann means all that which is still linked to time, to real life, in the form of real possibilities. Of course, there is also the 'cognitive' or 'idealistic' phenomenon of possibility. However, 'possibility' as a matter of cognition only considers a part of all those conditions which are present in real life. The cognitive (idealistic) concept of possibility does, in fact, abstract from time by saying that 'this is possible' without taking into consideration the conditions which are offered by a present 'now'. And this is, as Sesemann explains, very different from what happens in the sphere of Being: "Hier hat die Behauptung, dass etwas möglich *ist*, notwendig einen zeitlichen Sinn, sie gilt für das eben akuelle Jetzt [Here the statement that something *is* possible has a necessarily temporal sense, it is valid for the actual 'now']" (185).

Certainly, one of the roots of Sesemann's elaborations of Being which is characterized, through its relationship with a philosophical notion of possibility, as a dynamic, temporal Being, can be found in the philosophy of Hartmann. Hartmann also was trying to redefine the relationship between possibility and reality by claiming that what is 'real' does not necessarily exclude the existence of possibilities. On the contrary, possibility (*Möglichkeit*) is the counterpart of necessity, and *Wirklichkeit* (which Hartmann distinguishes from the scholastic notion of *Realität*) manifests its full richness of Being through a more sophisticated interplay of possibility and necessity.

Though Hartmann's complex treatment of this subject cannot be reproduced here in its entirety, one quotation from his comprehensive work *Möglichkeit und Wirklichkeit* might nevertheless illustrate the philosophical aim that was pursued by him:

> Von alter Tradition her ist ein Wirklichkeitsbegriff, der die inhaltliche Seinsfülle, oder die konkrete Bestimmtheit als Wirklichsein bezeichnet. Nach ihm stuft sich der Modus mit der Höhe der Seinsbestimmung ab: der Organismus gilt als 'wirklicher' als das leblose Ding, das seelische Wesen für

'wirklicher' als der Organismus u.s.f.; dieser Wirklichkeitsbegriff nähert sich dem scholastischen Realitätsbegriff, nach dem Gott das ens realissimus ist, weil er Inbegriff aller positiven Prädikate ist. Da man 'real' und 'wirklich' nicht unterschied, so sprang diese Bedeutung der realitas auf die Wirklichkeit über.

Since olden times there exists a notion of realness (*Wirklichkeit*) which characterizes as 'real' the content-oriented fullness of Being, or concrete determination. The mode of the amount of Being is graded according to this notion: the organism is more 'real' than the lifeless thing, a being which has a soul is more 'real' than the organism, etc.; this notion of realness (*Wirklichkeit*) comes close to the scholastic notion of reality (*Realität*) according to which God, as the symbol of all positive qualities, is the *ens realissimus*. Because 'real' and 'wirklich' were not distinguished, the realness (*Wirklichkeit*) is contaminated by this meaning of *realitas* (31).

Once again, we need to stress (and this time in the light of what has been said on Sesemann's thoughts about time and Being) the psychological relevance of some of these ideas. We have seen that, in keeping with Sesemann's anti-Freudianism, consciousness and unconsciousness are, in psychic Being, supposed to exist simultaneously and that a clear description of how the one could be determined by the other is neither possible nor useful. Finally this means that the "logic," 'necessity', or 'structure' of events or actions can be determined – even though these events or actions *might have* a link with a mental past – by crystallizing neither the logic of the objective present (in which the action took place) nor the subjective past (in which feelings, imaginations, etc. *did* exist). Instead the relationship between the spheres of the conscious and the unconscious respectively creates a dynamic of its own. We should have a closer look at how Sesemann describes this kind of dynamism.

As we have seen, Lossky was convinced that an artist can sometimes be surprised at his own work. The subjective content, once it is materialized in an *object* of art, can take the artist by surprise, just as if it were not himself who had effectuated the shift from subjective to objective Being. With Sesemann we are presented with a similar scheme of such a transfer, a scheme which clearly introduces new considerations into Freudian psychology. Sesemann is convinced

dass die Umsetzung von Willensregungen, Gefühlen, Stimmungen in Handlungen und Ausdrucksbewegungen nicht bloss einen Übergang, der den eigentlichen Gehalt des seelischen Erlebens gar nicht berührt, [darstellt], sondern dass hier mit diesem Übergang zugleich eine innere Umgestaltung Hand in Hand geht, welche das innere Erleben zu etwas anderem macht, ihm wesentlich neue Charaktere aufprägt. Nicht selten ereignet es sich, dass wir uns über unser eigenes Benehmen, unsere Handlungen, die aus einer bestimmten Stimmung hervorgegangen sind, wundern; sie scheinen uns durch diese Stimmung nicht genügend motiviert zu sein, und zwar nicht deshalb, weil in ihnen irgend welche unbewusste und daher für uns unerwartete Herzensregungen oder Triebimpulse zum Ausdruck kommen [...], sondern weil sie eine Eindeutigkeit und Bestimmtheit besitzen, die in der ursprünglichen Stimmung nicht lag, ja die ihr im Grunde wesensfremd war.

...that the transformation of wills, feelings, and moods into actions and movements of expression does not represent a transfer by which the contents of psychic experience remains unconcerned, but that, going hand in hand with this transfer, there is an inner process of reworking, a process which changes inner experience itself and which imposes new characteristics on it. It is not unusual for us to wonder at our own behavior, at actions which have risen from a certain mood; these behaviors or actions appear to be insufficiently motivated, and this not because they manifest unconscious (and thus unexpected) emotional movements or impulsions or drives [...]; it is simply because their unequivocalness and determination are much stronger than the original mood would have suggested, which was, properly speaking, different from them in its essence (*Die logischen Gesetze*: 97).

What happens through this interplay of subjective and objective is that new, dynamic rules are created, rules which no longer permit the determination of 'motivations' (subjective or objective ones), but which seem to follow a 'logic of their own'. This logic no longer appears as 'necessary' from some neutral point of view, a point of view that, for example, could have been established through a logic of Being. On the contrary, logic itself depends here to a very large extent on *contingency*; however, this contingency turns, as soon as it is spelled out in the form of rules of the subjective, into a logic of a very necessary kind. Human action can be seen as coming about in this way, and thus action always arises from a contingent (though at the same time logical) interplay of psychic and real life.

Naturally, such actions sometimes appear to us, if we try to see them in this way, very much like games. They do so because of their openness which is obviously derives from a certain degree of *contingency*; and because, at the same time, the whole 'organism' through which the action is represented seems to be 'closed' through certain inner necessity.

It might be helpful to refer, once again, to Lacan because for him too the 'coincidences' by which the subjective will appears at times to be 'fractured' are still, as he has insisted very often, linked to some kind of logic. In other words, in subjective life nothing happens '*comme au hasard*'; however, a 'necessity' cannot be introduced from the outside either:

> C'est à quoi nous, analystes, ne nous laissons jamais duper, par principe. Tout au moins, nous pointons toujours qu'il ne faut pas nous laisser prendre quand le sujet nous dit qu'il est arrivé quelque chose qui, ce jour-là, l'a empêché de réaliser sa volonté, soit de venir à la séance. Il n'y a pas à prendre les choses au pied de la déclaration du sujet [...]. C'est là le mode d'appréhension par excellence qui commande le déchiffrage nouveau que nous avons donné des rapports du sujet à ce qui fait sa condition.

> On that point, we, the analysts, cannot, in principle, be deceived. At the least we always point out that one should not be taken in when the subject tells us that something has happened which, on this particular day, prevented him from exercising his will, for example not to come to the session. Of course one should not take these declarations for granted [...]. It is the mode of apprehension *par excellence,* which suggests the new reading that we have given, of the relationships between the subject and that which constitutes its condition (*op. cit.*, 54).

Furthermore, for Sesemann the 'Unbestimmtheit' (which is as characteristic of manifestations of psychic life as dream is) is arbitrary and contingent only from a point of view which is settled outside of psychic life (or from the point of view of non-dream). In itself, however, it represents a necessary phenomenon. In this way, the life of being awake is clearly likened to the life of dream. The logic (of actions) is no longer a matter of (non-dreamt) Being, but depends "only" on our state of consciousness. In any case, an evaluation of the logic of dream on the grounds of the logic of real life is impossible. Or, in other words, the logic of real life is no more "true" nor more efficient than the logic of dream.

What is decisive here is that, though the detection of the particular relationship which exists between them, not only logic but also psychic Being receive a new character. This means that the logic of psychic Being is constituted by an '*Unbestimmtheit*' and this state of non-determination is a psychic fact; and it is a fact which cannot be changed through a change of our consciousness. In this way, once again, an apparent "contingency" can be declared a necessity. Sesemann writes:

> All diese Erwägungen verfolgen nur den einen Zweck: zu zeigen, dass die Unbestimmtheit, die sich an den Vorgängen und Gebilden des Innenlebens kund gibt, nicht etwas Belangloses und Zufälliges ist, nicht ein Scheinphänomen, das bloss der empirischen Enge und Beschränktheit des Bewusstseins sein Dasein verdankt, bei tiefgehender Betrachtung aber dagegen in Nichts zerrinnt, sondern dass es sich um eine wesenhafte Eigenheit des Psychischen handelt, die für seine ontologische Charakteristik und für sein Verhältnis zu den logischen Prozessen von fundamentaler Bedeutung ist.

> All these considerations have only one purpose: to show that the non-determinedness which manifests itself through the events and figurations of psychic life, is not irrelevant and contingent, not a sham phenomenon which owes its existence merely to the narrowness and limitations of consciousness, and will dissolve into nothing on closer scrutiny. On the contrary, we are confronted here with an essential quality of the psychic, a quality which is fundamental to its ontological characteristics and relationship with logical processes (105).

Conclusion

We have seen that Sesemann, in a very comprehensive way, elaborates an aesthetics of Being which produces unconventional ideas of time (as a concrete, dynamic phenomenon), of contingency (as a constitutive part of Being), and of structure which is seen as unformalizable in an either subjective or objective way. Sesemann's entire philosophical work, one might say, culminates in a new aesthetics of that domain within which all these factors play an equally prominent role in regard to their respective theorization: Sesemann's work culminates in a new *logic of dream*.

The dynamical aspect of all timely actions in which logical rationality would be present, is, as Sesemann says, in a "more relaxed" (*gelockert*) way also relevant for subjective Being. Among all the devices which have been suggested by Sesemann concerning the prevention of an undue objectivization of the subjective, there is one which appears as remarkably Heideggerian and Bakhtinian. Subjective, psychic Being should, as Sesemann declares, always be defined as a *Mitbewusstsein* (co-consciousness) which cannot be logically formalized. This means that subjective life should only be seen as appearing through a social aspect of non-determination; and only through this aspect does subjectiveness receive a temporal character:

> Eine Sonderstellung nimmt das eigentlich *subjektive* (psychische) Sein ein. Seine ursprüngliche Seinsweise (soweit sie einsichtig wird) ist die des *Mitbewusstseins*. Das Mitbewusstsein liegt aber noch diesseits aller Gegenständlichkeit. Als Mitbewusstes ist das psychische Sein daher ein *Vorgegenständliches*. Da aber logische Bestimmtheit an Gegenständlichkeit gebunden ist, so steht das psychische Sein als solches in keiner direkten Beziehung zu den logischen Gesetzen.

The *subjective* (psychic) Being occupies an exceptional position. Its original way of Being (as far as it is recognizable) is that of *co-consciousness*. But co-consciousness still exists beyond all objectiveness. Psychic being is therefore, as the co-conscious, pre-objective. However, because logical determination is linked to objectiveness, psychic Being maintains no direct relationship with the laws of logic (216).

The existence of a certain "logic of the psychic," of the subjective and of dream is explained, paradoxically, through a "pre-objective" link with what can be located *outside of the individual consciousness*. The myth of individual *subjectiveness*, as far as it neglects its own state of Being-in-the World, thus creates an unreflected idea of *objectiveness* that it claims, subsequently, to be valid within the domain of the subjective. The estrangement (*Entfremdung*, cf. 202) of man from the world is to a very large extent effectuated through such an abstraction from the (co-conscious), concrete, subjective contents of psychic life; and it always functions – though in a hidden way – through a scientific objectification.

Notes

1. V.N. Voloshinov - M.M. Bakhtin: *Freidizm: kriticheskij ocherk* [1927] (New York, 1983), pp. 30. Engl trans.: *Freudianism: A Marxist Critique* (New York, San Francisco, London: Academic Press, 1976), 19

2. Sesemann: "Über gegenständliches und ungegenständliches Wissen" (Kaunas: Lietuvos universiteto Humaitariu mokslu fakultetu rastai, 1927), 74.

3. Since the term *Selbstellung* does not exist in German and since we have no indications that would show Sesemann's intentions to create a neologism, we suppose that Sesemann wanted to formulate something like *Selbststellung*.

4. J. Lacan: *Les quatre concepts fondamentaux de la psychanalyse: Le séminaire, Livre XI*, 1964 (Paris: Seuil, 1973), pp. 37.

5. Medvedev mentioned once those thinkers whom he (in a slightly misleading way) as "evropejskij formalistyi" (European formalists) and who could be included here: Meier-Graeffe, Fiedler, Hildebrand, Worringer, and Riegl. *Formalistyi v literaturoprovedenii* (Leningrad: Priboi, 1928), 63. Engl. trans.: *The Formal Method Literary Scholarship*, Cambridge MA, Harvard University Press, 1985), 48. Walzel should certainly be added to the list.

6. Sesemann: "Das Logisch-Rationale" [Beiträge zum Erkenntnisproblem III] in *Eranus* I. Kaunas: Metai, 1930).

7. Cf. V.N. Voloshinov: *Marxism and the Philosophy of Language* (New York, London, Ann Arbor: Seminar Press, 1973), 11: "Idealism and psychologism overlook the fact that itself can come about only within a kind of semiotic material [...], that *itself can arise and become a viable fact only in the material embodiment of signs*. The understanding of a sign is, after all, an act of reference between the sign and other, already known signs; in other words, understanding is a response a sign with signs." Russian: *Marksizm i filosofia jazika* (Leningrad, 1928), 15.

8. Cf. Lacan in *De la psychose paranoïaque dans ses rapports avec la personnalité* (Paris: 1975) who is divergent on the point concerning the identification of psychic with *knowledge* but who manifests another clear parallelism with Sesemann: "On tend trop en effet, dans l'étude das symptômes mentaux de la psychose, à oublier sont des *phénomènes de la connaissance* et que, comme tels, ils ne sauraient être sur le même plan que les symptômes physiques" (338).

9. Sesemann: "Zum Problem der logischen Paradoxien" in *Eranus* III (Kaunas: Metai, 1935).

10. Sesemann: "Die logischen Gesetze und das Sein" (Kaunas: Metai, 1931) [*Eranus* II], 92.

11. Cf.: J Wortis: *Soviet Psychiatry* (Baltimore: William & Wilkins, 1950), p. 40: "[Pavlov's] teaching is said to affirm the fundamental theme of Marxism that social experience is the primary stuff of mind, and that the consciousness of man is a reflection of surrounding. His name is also coupled with Michurin as products of Russian materialist science, and of the practical realism of socialist culture, in contrast to the Morganists and Freudians of the West. "Pavlov," said Frolov, "destroyed Freud's house of cards." The disparaging criticism of Pavlov by some Western scientists and the general neglect of Pavlovianism is regarded in the USSR as additional evidence of the prevailing antagonism of Western science to an uncompromising and consistent materialist approach to life." Cf. also Jean Marti: "La psychanalyse russe" in *Critique* 346, March 1976, and E. Roudinesco: *J. Lacan & Co* (Chicago: Chicago University Press, 1990), p. 41ff.

12. N. O. Lossky: *The World as an Organical Whole* (Oxford: Oxford University Press, 1928), p. 36. Cf. Sesemann: 105: "Den theoretischen Betrachtungen über das Unbewusste liegt gewöhnlich die stillschweigende Voraussetzung zu grunde, den ihm zugehörigen Inhalten käme die gleiche Struktur zu, wie den Erlebnissen der Bewusstseinssphäre. Und da diese letzteren nach der Art gegenständlicher Phänomene behandelt werden, so erscheint es ganz selbstverständlich, auch dem Unbewussten die gleiche Gegen-ständlichkeit zuzuschreiben." 106: "... wenn Freud die ins Unbewusse verdrängten Regungen, Ideen und Vorstellungen mit Menschen vergleicht, die draussen an der verschlossenen Tür eines Hauses pochen und bei jeder Gelegenheit, wo die Tür unbewacht bleibt, in den Innenraum einzudringen suchen und die Bewohner desselben belästigen, - so leisten diese Räumlichen Bilder, so sehr sie in gewisser Hinsicht einen phänomenalen Tatbestand treffend charakterisieren, doch der irrtümlichen Ansicht vorschub."

13. N. Hartmann: *Kleinere Schriften III* (Berlin: De Gruyter, 1958), p. 369.

14. Sesemann: "M. Heidegger: Sein und Zeit" [Review] in *Mysl* (Paris: 1927). Sesemann must have been aware of the importance that this critique of "abstract intuitionism" has had in contemporary Germany. His characterization of intuitionism as the reverse side of "abstract

positivism" reads like an evocation of Oskar Walzel's main argument in his influential book *Das Wortkunstwerk*: "Denn die Intuition, die in sich selbst verharrt und sich darauf beschränkt, ihre begriffliche Unfassbarkeit und Unsagbarkeit zu behaupten, bleibt nicht nur unfruchtbar für die Erkenntnis, sondern schlägt auch unvermeidlich in ihr Gegenteil – die leere Abstraktion um." (*Die logischen Gesetze*: 159)

15. N. Hartmann: "Zeitlichkeit und Substanzialität" in *Kleinere Schriften I* (Berlin: De Gruyter, 1957), p. 202.

16. N. Hartmann: *Möglichkeit und Wirklichkeit* (Berlin: De Gruyter, 1966), p. 50.

Chapter 4

Intuition and Ontology in Sesemann and Bergson: Zeno's Paradox and the Being of Dream

1. Introduction

Vladimir Jankélévitch once said that Bergson could easily have "recognized himself in the realism of Lossky [as well as] in the immediacy of Frank" (Jankélévitch 1959: 2). An obstinate research for a certain "unity of spirit" to be found in the '*sobornost*' of Trubetzkoy as well as in S. Frank and Russian slavophilism, represents, according to Jankélévitch, the main driving force of Bergson's philosophy. For a long time, in Western Europe, Jankélévitch's statement could appear as "exotic," because almost no research into Bergson's reception in Russia had been done. Through the recent publications by Nethercott and Fink about Bergson's influence on Russian Modernism (1900–1930), Bergson's role in Russia has become much clearer.

   As a pupil of Lossky, Sesemann developed organic intuitionism by reflecting its "spiritualism" against the particular tasks that a typically modern Western European philosophy should face. As Hilary Fink has shown, Bergson's ideas concern Russian Modernism's "neo-Romantic preoccupation with artistic intuition" (Fink: 19) as much as Post-Symbolist movements like Acmeism and Futurism. Sesemann was not only a pupil of Lossky but, as a friend of Victor Zhirmunsky, had close contacts with the Russian formalist scene. Correspondingly, in Sesemann, those Losskian thoughts that are most reminiscent of Bergson develop into something more "formal." I want to show here how the idea of intuition develops in this Russian philosopher to some extent in parallel with Bergson's, but how, in

In 1957 with wife Wilma

the end, Sesemann was bound to cling to more hermeneutic motives. Like Bergson, Sesemann questions the "timeless" character of "objective" knowledge as it is guaranteed by natural sciences; but, contrary to Bergson, he is not ready to establish intuitionism as a method able to grasp living reality.

Further on I will show in which way an opposition of hermeneutic ontology to a realism of immanence becomes particularly interesting when both philosophers, Bergson and Sesemann, examine the phenomenon of dream. Here their respective analyses of Zeno's paradox of the arrow are instructive: they explain a similar Seinsweise of dream or logic of dream flowing out of both intuitive philosophy and ontology.

2. Bergson in Russia

In Russia, Bergson's ideas, especially that of "immediate intuition," had been taken up very quickly by "spiritualist philosophy" (Lopatin and later Frank, Berdiaev and Serguey Askoldov), but they found a clear echo in the founder of Russian intuitivism, N.O Lossky. After Solovyov's death a real intuitionist school developed in Russia. In spite of incompatibilities between the two philosophers (which Finks examines in her book), Lossky can be seen as Bergson's most consistent follower. His notion of intuition, which he developed even before undergoing any of Bergson's influence, was later refined, by the open adoption of some of Bergson's ideas. In his *Intuitivnaja filosofija* Bergsona (Lossky 1914), Lossky agrees with Bergson on the possibility of immediately grasping an original reality which appears to him to be "organic" as opposed to mechanistic. Lossky's position comes close to that of Bergson, who, together with the French school of "positivistes spintualistes," (cf. Bréhier 1968) attempted to overcome Cartesian ideas of mechanism and dualism.

However, Bergson's influence in Russia was not restricted to intuitivism. J. Vietroff writes in an article dating from 1912 that Bergson's influence would be as important as that of Kant and, curiously, announces that social revolution could best be theoretically based on Bergson's philosophy – rather than on Kant's – because only Bergson's clarity of language could permit the avoidance of "sectarianism" within the revolutionary process (Vietroff 1912). Given this enthusiasm for Bergson's philosophy in Russia, it is not surprising that Bergson's influence can also be detected in Acmeism (Ruskino 1982) and especially in the development of formalism ideas (while young Russian "neo-Kantians" consistently excluded Bergson as a point of reference).

3. Sesemann and Bergsonism

Like another philosopher who is at least loosely linked to Lossky, namely Sesemann's friend Nicolai Hartmann, Sesemann, has certain points in common with Bergson. This is most obvious in a book which Sesemann published in 1931 in Kaunas, where he develops thoughts almost identical to those published by Bergson between 1903 and 1923 in articles (which appeared in 1934 as *La Pensée et le mouvant* though Bergson had initiated them already in 1896, in *Matière et mémoire*).[1] Before engaging in a Bergsonian reading of some of Sesemann's texts, however, it needs to be said that in Sesemann's works one looks for comprehensive references to Bergson himself in vain. This might show how much Bergson's thinking had penetrated Sesemann's intellectual environment via Russian philosophy. Sesemann was apparently aware of Bergson's earlier writings, probably of *Durée et simultanéité* and of his doctoral thesis *L'Idée de lieu chez Aristote* (1889) in which his critique of the metaphysical subordination of time to space already appears. The fact, however, that Sesemann does not refer to Bergson's work at all when analyzing for example Zeno's paradox, lets us suppose that he developed his thoughts independently from Bergson to a large extent and probably only under Losskian influence.

In an article dating from 1926, the eminent Russian-French sociologist G. Gurvitch claims that among the immediate adepts of Lossky and Frank, one must also mention Sesemann as one of the philosophers most closely linked to Russian intuitivism (Gurvitch 1928: 260). Bergson's project is to reconcile idealism and realism by interpreting the notion of *esprit* in a way which makes it distinct from those metaphysical theories that tend to imagine spirit as an ideal, abstract, form, into which concrete matter could be introduced as if into an empty space. Instead, Bergson suggests looking at matter as a composition of images (*ensemble d'images*) which are perceived within a certain duration. A metaphysical formalism based on a long tradition separates 'abstract form' (or 'abstract time') from concrete matter. As a consequence, all conceptions of the world derived from this tradition are that abstract matter will be transformed into signs or into representations which makes its introduction into an "empty," abstract structure of a systematized world too easy.

Both Bergson and Sesemann are dissatisfied with the vision of the "real world" or "life" as phenomena that are composed uniquely of absolutely necessary structures. Both insist that "life" is also constituted by a certain amount of contingency. However, this contingency is not causal-mechanical: contingency and necessity should form a dialectical unity, as Sesemann writes in 1931. The causal-mechanical vision of the world "recognizes only one sort of necessity – the causal one – as the only necessity that dominates in reality, and considers the contingent as a merely subjective category."[2] Sesemann's ideas approach here formalist formulations. For Sesemann, the "multilayeredness of Being" asks for an enrichment of the sense of necessity itself. While, for science, matter is no more than "what it is," in "life," as perceived and produced by human consciousness, matter is changeable and obliged to contingency as much as to necessity. Bergson writes along these lines that "la matière est nécessite, la conscience est liberté; mais elles ont beau s'opposer l'une l'autre, la vie trouve moyen de les reconcilier" (BS: 14).

There are, as mentioned, few "official" points of contact between Bergson and Sesemann, which means that Sesemann does not appear to have had the intention of deriving concrete elements from Bergson's thought. Still there are obvious parallels with regard to approaches towards the philosophical definition of time, being and matter. Interestingly, in all of these points, Sesemann comes as close to Bergson as he does to Shklovsky and Tynianov. It is in the context of an analysis of Russian formalism that Sesemann declares that matter would be an artistic factor and therefore as "formal" as the form of an artwork itself. Matter and form would represent a unity and neither half would be more "necessary" or more "possible" than the other:

> [T]he composition is the formal moment, as are all factors which are obliged to the nature of the material itself. The structural form is not coined by the artist through the process of elaboration of the material [...] but materializes and reveals only aesthetic possibilities which are already living in the material itself, which are rooted in its intrinsic nature (Sesemann 1927: 187).

Sesemann wants the construction of the "aesthetic" (or even of thought itself) to be "thingly" because for any "authentically" creative art there is no irreconcilable dualism between the formal and the thingly-thought" (ibid.: 194). Like another philosopher from the Baltic region, his friend Nicolai Hartmann, Sesemann insists that matter is "irrational" and that it cannot be "rationalized" by means of either subjectivism or objectivism.

In spite of, or simply because of the Formalist context, the problem thus appears to be typically "Bergsonian." Hartmann writes that, in general, we all too easily consider "principles" to be rational, "matterless" (stoffreie), qualities which exhaust themselves all alone by becoming abstract relations. As a consequence, matter is conceived in contrast to precisely this: "When principles are rational they can indeed be a matter of thinking, of judgment and therefore of consciousness; whereas matters and substracts are opposed to this."[3] Still, this calculus is wrong because Hartmann also considers life itself to be "irrational" (ibid.) and there is no reason for man to believe that the limits of his *Seiende* would overlap with the limits of his thinking. Interestingly, the word "Formalism" appears, in Hartmann's in a negative sense. What collapses for Hartmann (as well as for Bergson) is a certain formalism (*Formalismusthese*). This is the very formalism on which both realism and idealism tend to build their ontological hypotheses.[4]

An encounter of Bergson and Sesemann takes place in the field of correspondences existing between Bergson's spiritualism and Sesemann's personal development of what he extracted from Losskian intuitionism. This encounter takes place at the moment both philosophers decide not to give in to any ontological reductionism which reproduces the world as either an individual or a general phenomenon. For Bergson, being and non-being can be mixed, simply because they are mixed in life as well as in our minds. We only need to admit that the material world is composed of images, and we will automatically see that no image can appear alone but that it always maintains relations with other images (cf. MM: 19–20). This aspect of Bergson's work – which could, in fact, be called hermeneutic – is present in Sesemann in the form of a more outspokenly hermeneutic project.

Gilles Deleuze has said that Bergson's method is called intuitionism and the problems which flow from such a methodisation of what seems to be opposed to method by its very nature, are obvious. However, the very problems which arise if we use intuition as a method for gaining knowledge, seem to be solved by Bergson even before they can arise: the Bergsonian "distribution" of the process of intuition over a certain timely period (*durée*) effectuates a shift of our philosophical interest, away from that which has so far been called "empathy," and confronts us with phenomena like "habits" which appear as habits not only of the mind but also as habits of the body or of a certain "style" adopted in real life. The "immediacy" of perception preserves only its positive aspect, but abandons the preponderant drawback of being timeless, static or even pantheistic.

Lossky's intuitionism does not seem to be aware of certain dangers inherent in any overtly "spiritual thinking." It is his pupil Sesemann who, when confronted with the constellation of elements inherited from his master, refers to solutions that are reminiscent of Bergson's. Lossky's intuitionism attempts to overcome Lipps' philosophy of *Einfühlung* (empathy), which, whenever confronted with the problem of perception, believes in nothing other than the perceiving self as a regulative instrument. Lossky insists on the importance of an "immanent theory of memory

(Lossky 1928: 43)," which would be able to conceive the self as a supra-temporal entity. Lossky clearly points to Bergson's idea of an "inter-penetration of past, present, and future" (86) in order to describe – though not develop – this theory of memory. Lossky recognizes that, even if we believe in our "own mind" as the only instance providing knowledge of the world, the images that we perceive will have a reduced character be-cause, "generally speaking, our mind is used to the impoverished world of our own conventional presentations" (128). Instead, he suggests perceiv-ing the world as an organic whole by reproducing it, in the subject's consciousness and through the very act of remembering, as an immanent vision of the world.

Lossky's idea is, of course, not just to follow the "habits of the mind." On the contrary, one needs to understand that subjectivism and empiricism are here criticized simultaneously, because empiricism also finds the "objectivity" of the world in nothing other than the habits of the subjective mind. This thought is developed by Sesemann who criticizes that empiricism would in this way objectify even the subjective mind: "The objectivity of the world of things, and its lawful order, is traced back to habits of the consciousness: in spite of this turn towards the subjective and the psychological, the main attitude of Hume's theory of knowledge remains objective."[5]

4. Zeno's Paradox

Subjective habits are more than abstract rules, and simply because of this, a habit cannot be transformed into an objective fact. A habit is "spiritual" in the same way in which being is spiritual, and it cannot be reduced to something objective (gegenständlich). Nothing is objective, not even matter, because the world is not perceived by a subjective consciousness: "The material Being as well as the organic one (life) is in its immediate appearance nothing less than being-conscious or thinking" (Sesemann 1927: 207). Bergson would say that the present world (through its prolon-gation into the past) is imagined. A rejection of all acts of "immobiliza-tion" (objectivization) of a world which exists within a time flow of phe-nomena is common to both Bergson and Sesemann.

Sesemann and Hartmann adhered to a "gnoseological idealism" which was supposed to break with both the subjectivist and positivist tra-dition. While Bergson developed a scientifically elaborated "realism of immediacy," gnoseological idealism decided to present its philosophy of immediacy in the form of an ontological metaphysics. Being methodol-ogically based on nothing other than a continuous movement that offers no "points fixes," one could say that a certain moment of "hermeneutic non-foundation" is common to both philosophies. What remains for Bergson an intuitive *"durée,"* becomes for Sesemann a "subjective *Erlebnis* of the concrete." The ground for "gnoseological idealism" was prepared by Lossky, and Bergson could have constructed his "intuitive realism" on the selfsame ground, as Jankélévitch wrote: "Des idées analogues forment le fond de la gnoséologie 'intuiviste' que professe le philosophe russe Nicolas Lossky. Comme Bergson, Lossky proteste contre un substantialisme grossier qui déracine irrémédiablement l'évidence de la perception et de la connaissance toute entière" (101–102). It is Sesemann who moves away, from Lossky as well as from Bergson, by radicalizing Bergson's claim about perception.

Sesemann recognizes the essential difference between knowledge and being, and that no knowledge of an object could ever be the object itself.[7] Intuitivism would be right, according to Sesemann, to contest natural science's right to be the only form of knowledge. However, and here Sesemann mentions Bergson, it would be questionable if intuitivism were also to have the right to establish "next to the naturalistic knowledge another one [...] which does not repose upon conceptual-analytical thinking but on a living intuition which grasps immediately the whole of the object" (Sesemann 1935: 75ff).

1960 at home

To Sesemann, any division of a lifeworld into a "logical" half which has only supra-temporal qualities and an empirical half which is temporal-historical does not make sense.[8] Any supra-temporal identity of things remains abstract and undetermined. Empiricism, on the other hand, is equally given to abstraction, because it does not presuppose the existence of material, but only of data which it will insert into abstract laws.

However, form and matter form a unity, and both – even matter – have a dynamic character: "The form or structure of the nature event [...] is intimately combined with the 'matter' of the real and therefore also more or less changeable" (Sesemann 1931: 130).

The Bergsonian character of these reflections is obvious. As already mentioned, there are, in general, few references to Bergson's work in Sesemann. In one of his main books, *Die logischen Gesetze und das Sein* (which appeared in the form of two articles in the same issue of the journal *Eranus*), Sesemann criticizes the metaphysical and scientific reduction of the dynamic, temporal component of movement. There is no explicit reference to Bergson's treatment of the subject, though Sesemann analyses Zeno's classical paradox of movement almost in parallel with Bergson. In a footnote that appears in the first part of the book (thus not in the part in which Zeno's paradox is treated), Sesemann mentions Bergson as one of the representatives who, together with Heidegger and Scheler, would have defined "perception" as not a purely theoretical act but who would have insisted, by seeing contemplation as a kind of transformation, on the involvement of perception with practical life (79 note 14).

Bergson believes that metaphysics started at the very moment Zeno of Elea pointed to a contradiction with regard to movement and change, saying that a movement that takes place within a certain period of time is at the same time no movement because it is possible to divide a time period into instants, and to state that within these instants there would be no movement at all. The aporia consists in saying that it is the instant which determines time, though, at the same time, the instant is not part of the time movement. In *La Pensée et le mouvant* Bergson criticizes Zeno for his intellectualist vision of time. From Zeno on, Greek philosophers confronted with similar paradoxes would react by looking for "reality" only within a domain existing outside (or beyond) time. Metaphysics, which for Bergson came into being on the very day on which Zeno pronounced his paradox, would be unable to recognize that "what is real [...] is the flux" (cf. 5–7) For Bergson, Zeno's motivation for his mischievous act was that he would refuse to perceive time "with his senses." Instead of seeing time as a combination of movement and matter, he would fully give in to "supra-sensible" explanations which reproduce the notion of time in terms of "ideas" or other abstractions, (cf. 146) Plato would have been the first to look for "la réalité cohérente et vraie dans ce qui ne change pas" (156).

For Bergson movement is real, and, he declares in the last pages of *Matière et mémoire*, it can be perceived immediately without our having to reorganize it intellectually by means of our spirit (by trying, for exam-

ple, to construct movement by lining up several "non-moving" moments).
It is Zeno's fault to have thought of time like space, i.e. as a unity which
can be divided in smaller and smaller parts. However: "Le mouvement
immédiatement perçu est un fait très clair, et [...] les difficultés ou les
contradictions signalées par l'école d'Elée concernent moins le mouvement lui-même qu'une réorganisation artificielle, non viable, du mouvement par l'esprit" (MM: 215).

Sesemann also regrets (in a way which is more than reminiscent of
Bergson) the "spatialization" of time which he crystallizes in Zeno's
paradox. What happens in Zeno is a "Re-interpretation of the dynamics of
movement as static-spatial being."[9] In this way "real matter" is lost or, as
usual in science, only referred to as an *Urstoff*, i.e. an abstraction which
exists beyond any temporality (66), Sesemann tends to recognize Zeno's
paradox as a necessary "irrationality," which should not be neutralized by
physics. More precisely, physics would not even neutralize it, but only
cover it by means of a sophisticated logical interpretation. Sesemann
claims a recognition of the "non-validity of logical laws for the sphere of
the temporal event [...] as far as these laws are linked as particularly logical laws to the static aspect and cannot grasp the dynamics of becoming."[10] This is no different to Bergson's thesis about Zeno, which consists
in recognizing that the whole of a time period on the one hand, and its
divisions on the other, form only one time (Sesemann 1935: 32). Only the
flux of notions can provide a coincidence of the "becoming of the thing
and the becoming of thinking"[11] I will show below that it is questionable
whether intuition – even a 'fluent' one – is, for Sesemann, the right means
to produce such a coincidence. In general, Sesemann believes that Hegel
would have better recognized the significance of reflexive reason than
Bergson, by using a dialectical model (Sesemann 1935: 40).

The intellectual encounter of Sesemann and Bergson takes place
because both philosophers work on the redefinition of the process of perception, which, in the opinion of both, needs to be reinvented by avoiding
the timeless character that has so far been granted to perception by a philosophy which equates perception with instantaneous intuition. Both
Sesemann and Bergson recognize that "abstraction" means "spatialization," and this is the reason why both come across the paradox of Zeno.
However, the paths of Sesemann and Bergson are bound to separate at
some point (though not for good) because their general intentions were
different. Still, their encounter provides the possibility of drawing comparisons that could otherwise not be made so easily. It is clear that, in the
end, a critique of Zeno is for Sesemann a matter of ontology. He comes
close here to Lossky's successor S. Frank, who modified Lossky's metaphysics of intuition into a more ontological theory of knowledge. For

Bergson, on the other hand, Zeno's problem is one of realism, which is adapted to a dynamis which, after all, remains scientific. For Sesemann, it is the concrete *Ding* in an almost Heideggerian sense that is present in the centre of his considerations. For Bergson it is a *matière* which is involved into a dynamical game of perception in which our memory as well as our body participate.

Sesemann wants to combat the "predominance of the static-spatial aspect over the temporally-dynamic one," in order to enable the perception of "an original conception of environmental Being" ("ursprüngliche Auffassung des umweltlichen Seins," 66). Bergson's alternative, on the other hand, is a "past-present" which is "played by matter and imagined by spirit" (MM: 251). Here we are obviously confronted with a perception which plays along the lines of the hermeneutic circle, and which declares that "la connaissance de la vie doit être une imitation de la vie" (Jankélévitch: 74). The question is whether both approaches – Sesemann's and Bergson's – are compatible or whether they are radically opposed to each other.

5. Dream, Intuition and Ontology

This question, whether a hermeneutic ontology and a realism of immanence have aims in common, cannot, of course, be fully answered in this article. It seems, however, that the bifurcation as which separated Bergson and Sesemann at one point does not inaugurate a finality. As a matter of fact, both philosophers meet again when ontological and intuitive-realistic approaches lead them to a consideration of the phenomenon of dream.

Philosophies of non-foundation, which renounce fixed points in the presence in order to give the status of reality to an eternal flow, must explain the relationship between dream and reality in a special way. Aristotle, when considering Zeno's paradoxes, preferred to simply neutralize them because he was convinced that they would lead him into a dangerous sphere between being and non-being. Another of Zeno's paradoxes about space, which claims that any space would be contained in another space and so forth (Zeno A 24), is rejected by Aristotle (Phys. IV, 3, 210b 22) as illogical for the same reason. The intermediary sphere between being and non-being, a sphere founded on a paradoxical thought that cannot be placed within a logical system, is like a dream. As a consequence, a re-evaluation of this sphere of dream has been undertaken by Sesemann as well as by Bergson. Both Sesemann and Bergson insist on a certain redefinition of the meaning of the "undetermined." Whereas for metaphysics, reality and dream, consciousness and unconsciousness form two separate entitles between which lines of correspondence can be established by means of analysis, both Sesemann and Bergson plead for a dynamic concept of reality which is constituted by images providing a synthesis of the conscious and the unconscious. Though Sesemann does not use the word "image," it is likely that it would have suited him because of his opposition to the idea of a Vergegenständlichung (objectivation) of dynamic elements. Any objectivizing thought necessarily produces spatial metaphors, because *Gegenstände* (objects) are supposed to be contained within a space. Indeed, it is a spatial metaphor which bothers Sesemann, this time with regard to dream. Metaphysical, static conceptions of reality tend to see waking life (as well as consciousness) as a closed "space," within which non-moving elements (objects) can be considered. Dream or unconsciousness would exist within a similar space. In particular, Sesemann criticizes Freud's images of "emotions repressed into the unconscious" ("ins Unbewußte verdrängten Regungen") which would try to penetrate into the "interior" ("Innenraum") of consciousness. The spatial, static separation of dream and reality leads to the tacit acceptance that in "reality" perceptions are clear, determined and intense, whereas for dream the opposite is true. Dream appears as a pale version of waking life. The deconstruction of this opposition represents a philosophical aim shared by Bergson and Sesemann.

For Sesemann it is rather the abstract world of scientific laws which is unbestimmt, whereas the world of dream is clear (cf. "Das Problem der logischen Paradoxien," 83). This means that dream has its own *Seinsweise* and its own logic; "The problem [of dream images] that we are considering overlaps neither with non-clarity nor with the confusion of memorized images or imaginations."[12]

Similarly, for Bergson, "Le rêve a toute apparence de la réalité" (PM: 125). If we are looking for a "determinateness" which could guarantee us that we are awake and not dreaming at a given moment, we should remember that already Descartes decided that such a certitude is not available. Bergson's thoughts about dream run in parallel to his philosophy of perception, and a quotation from Jankélévitch underlines the special status he gives to dream: "Les uns feraient volontiers du souvenir une perception affaiblie. Les autres traitent la perception comme un souvenir renforcé" (Jankélévitch: 97). However, dream and reality, perception and memory, belong to different spheres; and within each of these spheres experiences can be made with the same intensity. When Sesemann says that dream has its own *Seinsweise*, this is entirely Bergsonian, if we consider a statement from Jankélévitch; "Qu'on multiple le rêve par lui-même autant que l'on voudra, jamais on n'obtiendra la veille: ces deux mondes ne sont pas du même ordre, ils appartiennent à deux plans différents" (Jankélévitch: 99). The "place" in which dream takes place is different from that in which takes place reality. The logic of this place is as absolute as that of any place. Sesemann writes: "The originality of such dream images is that the logical non-determinedness here becomes a fact without being seen as nonsense or as an absurdity."[13]

Conclusion

One can only speculate whether the "clear" dreamsphere that Sesemann speaks of (and which is also considered by Bergson) corresponds to what Shklovsky thought of as "film" in his cinematic theory founded on Bergson. In any case, Sesemann's main intention is to question the objective (gegenständliche) perception which has established itself as the only one possible, through the authority of the natural sciences. Sesemann is convinced that any objective experience would only be a "partial experience." This is one of his main convictions, which speaks through many of his texts. The question Sesemann is trying to answer is whether intuition represents just another way of "objectification," or if it fully corresponds to the "essence of knowledge." Sesemann answers this question by denying intuition its positive aspect, which means that Bergson's, as Lossky's, and also Husserl's models of intuitive perception are rejected. What remains is a hermeneutically oriented knowledge which designates the act of knowing – in a circular way – as an act of self-knowledge. Only in this way can we neutralize the initial difficulty that any knowledge of a thing would not be the thing itself; "Knowledge is not only knowledge of a being different from itself but it is also knowledge of itself; it 'has' something else and itself. This constituted the wonder of its reflexitivty."[14]

    If Sesemann was interested in Zeno's paradox, then it is because the problem of the *chôra* itself questions objective thinking as such, since knowledge does always need to be different from the thing it knows: there is no absolute knowledge, because this knowledge would be nothing other than a knowledge of itself. "Intuitionism" seems to neglect this very problem, and believes that the "real object" could overlap with the object existing in consciousness, (cf. "Zum Problem des reinen Wissens, Schluß: 326–333) This is the reason why, in the end, intuitionism turns out to be another sort of objectivism. However, as Sesemann said in his inaugural lecture at Kaunas University: "The real object of philosophical knowledge is a being of a higher order, which is a concrete as well as a real one, just like the individual being of the knowing soul (of the subject) itself."[15]

Notes

1. Bergson's works quoted in this article: *Durée et simultanéité: A propos de la théorie d'Einstein* [DS] (Paris: Alcan, 1922); *La Pensée et le mouvant* [PM] (Paris: Quadrige 1987 [1934]); *L'Energie spirituelle: essais et conférences* [ESJ (Paris; Alcan, 1919); *L'Ideé de lieu chez Aristote* in Mélanges (Paris: Presses universitaires de France, 1972 [Alcan, 1889]); *Matière et mémoire* [MM] (Paris: Presses universitaires de France, 1997 [1896])

2. "[...] erkennt nur eine Art von Notwendigkeit – die kausale – als die in der Wirklichkeit allein herrschende an, und betrachtet das Zufällige als bloß subjektive Kategorie." "Die bolschewistische Philosophie in Sowjet-Rußland," 181. For Sesemann's ideas on contingency see also his review of August Faust's *Logik und Ontologie der Möglichkeit* in *Blätter für deutsche Philosophie* 10, Berlin 1937.

3. "Wenn Prinzipien rational sind, so können sie in der Tat Sache des Denkens, des Urteils, und folglich Sache des Bewußtseins sein, während Materien und Substrate sich dem sichtlich widersetzen." N. Hartmann: *Kleinere Schriften* II (Berlin: De Gruyter, 1957), 290– 91.

4. Some words on the role of formalism in this discussion are necessary. As is well known, Bergson's interpretation of Zeno's paradox has had considerable influence also on Russian Formalism and cannot go unmentioned here. Larissa Rudova speaks even of a "Bergsonian paradigm in Formalism" (Larissa Rudova: "Bergsonism in Russia: The Case of Bakhtin" in *Neophilologus* 80, 1996, 175–188, 177) which might explain why the idea of "form" repeatedly appears in Sesemann in contexts where one would not expect it. without pretending that intuitivism and Formalism would be phenomena of the same order, it is certain that Sesemann's case, since Formalist influences in his philosophy do exist, shows how much Bergson's philosophy can be seen as an element granting coherence to Russian Modernism. James H. Curtis has analyzed the Bergsonian basis of Formalism, which is manifest especially in Shklovsky's and Tynianov's theories. (James H. Curtis: "Bergson and Russian Formalism" in *Comparative Literature* 28 Spring 1976, 109–121). Shklovsky's discussion of Zeno's paradox of the arrow which does not move because I the space which it traverses is divided into infinitely smaller spaces, is adopted from Bergson: "Bergson has analyzed Zeno's paradox [...] which shows that movement is impossible. [...] Bergson has overcome the difficulty caused by Zeno by showing that we do not have the right to break movement into separate parts. Movement is continuous and, in Zeno's case, the movement itself is replaced with the way the body traverses during its movement" (Shklovsky in *Literatura i kinematograf*) (V. Shklovsky: *Literatura i kinematograf* (Berlin; 1923), p. 23). At the beginning of the twentieth century, the separation of form and matter released an immense potential for artistic exploration. Matter that was supposed to be "neutral" could function within contexts of extreme liberty. Bergson's efforts to bring form and matter together are shared by the Russian formalists, and also by Sesemann, who developed an aesthetics which is aware of experimental tendencies of early twentieth century art and linguistics. Finally, in Sesemann it culminates in the construction of a philosophy of Being which defines itself in opposition to several modern approaches and in this is even reminiscent of Heidegger.

5. Sesemann 1930: "Die Objektivität der Dingwelt und ihre gesetzmäßige Ordnung wird auf Gewohnheiten des Bewußtseins zurückgeführt. Trotz dieser Wendung ins Subjektive und Psychologische bleibt die Grundeinstellung der Humeschen Erkenntnistheorie dennoch eine gegenständliche" (p. 149–50).

6. Ibid., 184; "Das materiale Sein, ebenso wie das organische (das Leben), ist in seiner unmittelbaren Erscheinung nichts weniger als Bewußtsein oder Denken."

7. "...neben der naturalistischen Erkenntnis eine andere [...], die nicht auf diskursivem begrifflich-analytischem Denken beruht, sondern auf lebendiger das ganze des Gegenstandes unmittelbar erfassenden Intuition" (1927: 216).

8. "Die Form oder Struktur des Naturgeschehens [...] ist mit der 'Materie' des realen innerlich verwachsen und in sofern auch mehr oder weniger veränderungsfahig" (Sesemann 1935: 77).

9. "Nicht-Gültigkeit der logischen Gesetze für die Sphäre des zeitlichen Geschehens [...] insofern als diese Gesetze als spezifisch logische an den statischen Aspekt gebunden sind und daher die Dynamik des Werdens und Vergehens nicht zu fassen vermögen" (1927: 153).

10. Cf. Deleuze, *Le Bergsonisme* (Paris: Presses universitaires de France, 1966).

11. It is interesting to note that another of Zeno's paradoxes, namely that of the fleet-footed Achille and the tortoise, the logic of which is certainly closely linked to Zeno's paradoxes cited in this article, has repeatedly been interpreted as a dream (nightmare) metaphor. See on this subject George Devereux, *Dreams in Greek Tragedy* (Berkeley & Los Angeles; University of California Press, 1976), xxi and note 6.

12. "Das Problem [der Traumbilder], das wir ins Auge fassen, deckt sich weder mit Unklarheit noch mit der Verworrenheit von Erinnerungs und Phantasiebildern" ("Die logischen Gesetze": 91).

13. "Darin besteht die Eigentümlichkeit solcher Traumbilder, daß die logische Unstimmigkeit hier zur Tatsache wird, ohne jedoch als nonsens, als Absurdität einpfunden zu werden" ("Die logischen Gesetze": 92).

14. "Das Wissen ist nicht nur Wissen eines von ihm verschiedenen Seins, sondern auch das Wissen seiner Selbst; es 'hat' ein anderes und sich selbst. Darin besteht das Wunder seiner Reflexivität" ("Zum Problem des reinen Wissens": 230).

15. "Der wahre Gegenstand der philosophischen Erkenntnis ist vielmehr ein Sein höherer Ordnung und zwar ein ebenso konkretes und reales Sein, wie das individuelle Sein der erkennenden Seele (des Subjekts) selbst" ("Das Problem des Idealismus in der Philosophie": 115).

Socrates and the Problem of Self-Knowledge (1925)[1]

Vasily Sesemann

I

Though the subject of the present essay is purely technical, it nevertheless bears a close link with the most burning questions of modernity. The dangerous overvaluation that all European civilization is undergoing at the moment, asks for reconsideration of the problem of knowledge. Knowledge is indeed one of the main driving forces of our culture to which many people tend to ascribe a leading role. The analysis of the nature of knowledge should thus shed light on its role in all psychical and cultural life.

The problem of Socrates is one of the eternal problems of European civilization. In moments of spiritual crisis when all cultural achievements undergo revaluation and revision, when the sense and destiny of culture are questioned, European civilization is reborn, requiring deeper and more principal decisions. What is the way indicated by Socrates to European man? Is it true or false? And what is actually the meaning of the phenomenon Socrates? Are his teachings ultimately positive or negative? This problem arose first with the Christian apologists and Church fathers. Here appeared the distinction between two fundamental currents of Christian thought: the first one, negating all linguistic philosophy (and intellectual culture), and the other one, seeing in these the necessary preliminary step enabling the full development of Christian Truth. For Clement of Alexandria[2] as for all Platonizing patristic[3] schools, Socrates was the forerunner of Christianity and bearer of a natural revelation, manifesting itself in the truth of reason. In the eyes of Tertullian and his disciples, on the other hand, Socrates is one of those heretics manipulating those wicked "demons." He tries to seduce with his philosophy the Christian soul by inducing in them the idea of religious self-determination and finally causing their fall from the united truth of the Church. However, the problem of Socrates has, apart from its historical aspects, also another, timeless one. This concerns the significance of the intellectual foundation common to all spiritual and religious civilization. It unavoidably leads to the question about the relationship between faith and knowledge, a question to which are linked the most severe and deepest crises of Christian consciousness. Is it really possible to speak of the complete and unhealthy dissolution of faith in knowledge in the way in which the Alexandrians believed to have found it in the absolute gnosis?

Does the affirmation of the autonomy of knowledge really necessarily kill the life base of all faith?

The religious meaning of the problem of Socrates represents only one moment, one side, of the cultural significance of the entire problem. The first one who noticed this was Hegel, and he pointed to the destructive influence that Socrates' teachings had exercised on moral life and the sense of justice of his contemporaries. However, his own rationalism would then only block any access to the problem of Socrates in all its depth and complexity. Hegel sees in Socrates' intellectualism the highest form of the realization of a dialectically developing history.

Nietzsche poses the problem of Socrates in a more concrete way as he approaches it from the angle of art. Finally, this new approach permits him to see what Hegel and all those preceding Nietzsche had simply let slip away. In his eyes, Socrates' intellectualism is first of all the power negating and destroying the supreme achievement of the ancient soul, which is the tragic art of Aeschylos and Sophocles. The reason for this is that this destructive power is just that phenomenon which testifies the coming decline of civilization, the exhaustion of its creative forces, and the perversion of its vital sexual instincts.

Christianity became the religion of the European world only at the moment it had absorbed in itself the intellectual culture of the Ancients, and decided to use the achievements of Ancient philosophy for the renewal and development of Christian religious doctrines and *Weltanschauung*. However, the victory of these Alexandrian, synthesizing thoughts was far from fully achieved. Antirational tendencies subsisted in the Christian consciousness and with every new rise of religious life and religious creativity it awoke anew with strengthened forces. Even in such movements as the Reformation, which governed to a significant degree humanist aspirations towards the reasonable self-determination of the person, even in people whose nature was strongly religious (for example Luther), broke through at times a deep and perhaps instinctive distrust towards reason and its creative forces. And in the light of all this, can we really see in Tertullian's and likeminded people's severe judgment about Socrates' intellectualism not more than the fruit of fanatic blindness, not more than the non-understanding of authentic beings of ancient culture? Is this really simply a false identification of true philosophy with senseless and fruitless idle talk of the latest scholastic school against which the apostle Paul (*Colossian* II) protected his herd so persistently? And is it not significant that this ambiguous attitude towards knowledge that exists in Christian thought, manifests itself also in the mythological consciousness? Knowledge plays a decisive role in the fall of man, and it determines his historical and religious way towards redemption; of this speak both Greek myths and biblical narratives. However, the evaluation of the role of knowledge goes here in the opposite direction. In the Orphic myths the Fall expresses itself through the loss of knowledge, through the soul's forgetfulness of that Divine Beginning to which it is linked with all its essence, and to which it owes its entire Being and its mortality. The forgetfulness separates the soul from God and approaches it through mortality and corporeal being. The way of salvation is therefore the way of resurrection of that knowledge, the "recollection" (*pripominanie*) of what the soul had forgotten at the moment it fell. Only through knowledge the soul gets purified and acquires the capacity to unite itself anew with the Godly Origin. A completely different meaning is attached to knowledge by biblical tales. The knowledge of good and bad is a kind of imaginary good, for the sake of which the ancestors of mankind violated the godly commandment and exposed themselves to expulsion from Paradise. Namely the knowledge of good and bad does not assimilate man to God but, on the contrary, estranges man from Him. Instead of liberating him, it lets him fall into the slavery of sin.

How can one explain the opposition of these two religious concepts of knowledge? Certainly, one should not consider it as a simple coincidence and as a caprice of mythological imagination. However, if it is not coincidental, does it not reflect some objective opposition that is characteristic of real knowledge? Is it not the opposition of both of its sides or moments necessary, because both are to the same extent rooted in the very essence of its nature?

II

As the centre point of Socrates' philosophy appears, as is well known, the concept of the identity of the good and knowledge and – doubtless – the principal notion is here not the good but knowledge; knowledge does here not identify with the good but the good identifies with knowledge. From this is often concluded that Socrates' philosophical interests would concentrate on logical problems. Socrates, one says, is first of all the founder of logic; he was the first to inaugurate a purely logical reflection that is not limited to logical aims. His philosophical pathos was primarily and essentially the pathos of a fanatic addicted to abstracting logicism. When he dedicates his conversations to problems of moral and moral education, this is only in order to have a concrete historical support on the grounds of which he can reveal the logical essence of his thoughts. And self-knowledge (that is knowledge originating in the subject) is for him only one step on the stair leading to objective knowledge. Therefore Socrates is the forefather of those new, modern intellectuals or, more precisely, of scientific culture as a whole which subsequently acquired such a leading role in the development of all spiritual life in Europe.

However, this interpretation of Socrates' intellectualism is not only historically incorrect and contains aspirations to modernize his philosophical project, it fails to detect the most characteristic specificity of Socrates' intellectualism. The "purity" of Socrates' thought does not consist in the fact that it would have been freed of any content, but in the fact that it has a perfectly particular content: virtue itself and man itself as a whole. Because his logical notions are not self-sufficient they turn out to be entirely adequate attempts to formulate the authentically living and vital thought in his teaching. Socrates' concern is not in scientific development; he is governed by the care for man's soul and its moral accomplishment. And only out of this concern in man's soul will grow his teachings of logic, constantly maintaining an organic link with it. Otherwise the exclusive power of Socrates' influence on the destiny of the spiritual culture of the ancient and the European world would be incomprehensible. Incomprehensible would also be the link between his teaching and the most intimate motivations of Platonism.

Of course, the meaning of Socrates' logical discoveries expands itself beyond the borders of that moral being on which he focused his examinations, and it is therefore true that he also laid the foundation for abstract scientific thought. However, the living nerve of his philosophy is not limited to this, but resides rather in a unique combination and fusion of the notions of knowledge and the good, which he tried to express in the paradoxical formula of their inseparable unity and identity. And therefore only the interpretation of this formula as a whole can reveal the true idea of Socrates' intellectualism and lead to statements about his philosophical importance and about the new and lasting elements that he contributed to the spiritual life of mankind.

One often says that Socrates was the first to announce the autonomy of the foundation of moral. However, it goes without saying that the very notion of autonomy is not at all of ancient origin and is therefore far removed from any of Socrates' aspirations. It is ambiguous, giving rise to the following question: which kind of autonomy is it that Socrates discovers? And how must be seen its inner link with his notion of knowledge? Is not just in his intellectualism hidden a serious threat for moral autonomy? And does moral autonomy not get dissolved in the autonomy of knowledge? All complications linked to the notion of autonomy clearly prove that this notion cannot serve as a key to the understanding of Socrates' teaching. The solution of his secret must obviously be looked for in something else.

III

If we limit ourselves to the notions and thoughts with which Socrates was familiar, and if we try to crystallize their fundamental nucleus that later became the formula of the identity of the good and knowledge, then, so it seems, it is above all unavoidable to mention three points of his teaching: the opposition of authentic and apparent knowledge, the characterization of the true as object of the true knowledge, and the passage to true self-knowledge. Socrates opposes true knowledge (that he is searching for) to the imaginary and apparent knowledge of the sophist. This knowledge is imaginary but not false. The Sophists' knowledge is apparent because it is, in its essence, without object; it does not attain its object but gets stuck halfway in linguistic struggles, replacing the object – its appearance – with linguistic meaning that is not rooted in the object but remains floating, indeterminate and ghostly. To *logos* Socrates prefers the notion. The notion (понятие) is supposed to guarantee objectivity (обьективность), that means objectivity (предмедность) of knowledge; it is not through its generality – this moment is only secondary, formally-logical – but through the crystallization of knowledge in the notion, that the notion points to the object; it points to the object, to its essence, through its intention, though the question out of which it arises (what is this?). To the extent that it materializes itself generally, the notion actively grasps and seizes the object.

Therefore the objectivity of knowledge signifies the authenticity of its content. And the authenticity of this content is also the authenticity of reality. However, as is generally known, according to ancient philosophy, "the similar recognizes the similar." Therefore, in authentic knowledge exists also the authentic real object. However, this object is for Socrates just virtue, the good. It does not contradict knowledge as the most excellent of its content, as the transcendental of its object, but in it exists the authenticity (objectivity) of knowledge, signifying nothing other than the immediate presence of the authentic, that is authentically-real, object. This is the reason why authentic knowledge is simultaneously the good, meaning that it is identical with it.

We have thus revealed the link between Socrates' teaching and leading ideas of ancient gnoseology. But can this link justify and support the identity of the good and of knowledge? Is in this trait of Socrates' intellectualism not just hidden its fundamental drawback, is there not hidden just all those lifeless aspects of life that should be averted and overcome?

XX

The tragedy of knowledge has not been overcome by European culture even until today. It will not be overcome it as long as this culture does not changed itself, as long as it lodges in itself the legacy and the tradition of the Hellenistic-Christian *logos*. The question to be asked is: which meaning has knowledge in spiritual life today? What was its meaning until now, and what should it be in the present and in the future? The essence of this question has already been developed in the preceding analysis. Now we will talk about the form of knowledge of contemporary thought. Is it dominated by a being (бытийные) or a meonic[4] foundation? And in which direction should its forces be directed in order to neutralize and paralyze its force; in order to disarm and paralyze the destructive activity of meonic reason? In one way, so it would seem, contemporary European culture has passed by all preceding époques: it has seemingly finished with and irrevocably overcome intellectualism in all domains. It no longer believes in the real force of logical reason; just as antiquity, the middle ages, enlightenment and the idealist philosophy of Romanticism did not believe in it. However, looking a little deeper into this matter, this victory turns out to be only partial and not at all definitive. It is enough to look at those currents of socio-political thought that are dominant in our days, to convince oneself that rationalist temptations (even if they appear here in the disguise of a socialist and communist utopia), continue to confuse modern man. Apart from that, intellectualism has not adopted the unified form out of which could flow meonic, cultural tendencies.

Then there are also other, not less efficient and not less dangerous forms of intellectualism. As such appears for example contemporary Positivism. Positivism grants a leading role to positive science in culture. For Positivism, science means especially natural science that adopts an essentially objective (предметный) attitude and is based on the objective experiment. All other sciences, in order to become exact (i.e. "scientific" in the complete sense of the word), are obliged to assimilate themselves to natural sciences and, like them, accept the objective experiment as a basis and use corresponding (scientific) research methods. It could appear that the Positivist position, compared with any other point of view, presents an immense advantage. It concentrates only on facts, on pure experience in which apparently exists a particularly strongly developed feeling for reality, and in which meonic tendencies are apparently missing. However, these advantages of positivism develop in the best case within the "outer" sphere of the scientific (objective) experiment. When one tries to grasp Positivism in relation with psychic-spiritual Being, one should not fail to understand, that Positivism does not take very much into consideration the particularity of this realm, but violates with its methods of research its facts, for example rationalism.

Flowing out of purely objective orientations, positivism sees nothing but scientific facts. Other manifestations of reality (psychological-mental ones, for example), enter its horizon only to the extent to which they are assimilated to scientific facts, for example submitted to clarity. Only when positivism will gradually loose its dominant position in philosophy and psychology, it will become clear to which degree its narrow and one-sided understanding of reality has simplified, flattened and banalized psychic life by denying to face the deeper layers of Being. Positivism is not only a theory, and its overcoming within the domain of philosophy is not really decisive for its entire destiny. Bring more like a spiritual attitude corresponding to the lifestyle and life conception of modern European mankind, it conquers the intellect of the large masses, and is therefore particularly dangerous for the mental culture as a whole. Meonic tendencies peculiar to positivism are so powerful and have deeply entered the contemporary European soul that it threatens to become mutilated and to ultimately loose the ability to perceive a higher form of spirituality. [...]

Notes by the translator

1. Source: "Сократ и проблемы самознания" in *Evraziiskii Vremennik* 4:2 (Berlin: 1925), pp. 224–267, extracts.

2. Clement of Alexandria (born 140/150, died 216/217): Greek Christian philosopher who interpreted Greek philosophy as representing a preliminary stage leading to Christian faith. Had a strong influence on St. Augustine.

3. Between the 2nd and the 7th–8th centuries, patristic philosophy dealt with the philosophical heritage of Ancient Greek philosophy. Clement of Alexandria is a representative of Patristic philosophy.

4. The notion "meonic" is important in Russian philosophy of the nineteenth and early twentieth century, in particular in that of Berdiaev. Berdiaev defines man in relation to three worlds: the divine, the natural, and the meonic (diabolical). The meonic represents a "nothingness" in the sense of *me on* (as opposed to *ouk on*). Berdiaev bases his idea of "nothingness" especially on Jacob Böhme's notion of the *Ungrund* out of which the world was created, but which cannot be empty itself. The meonic *Ungrund* is irrational, free and full of potential, because not yet determined by God.

Appendix II

On the Nature of the Poetic Image (1925)[1]

Vasily Sesemann

I

The task of the present essay is to clarify some fundamental structural particularities of the poetic image that flow out of the very nature of poetic verse as much as out of the words of the verse. Furthermore, its task is to show that these particularities likewise determine those components that are normally considered the vehicle of the originality and aesthetic dignity of poetic speech: *intuition* (in the broadest sense of the word).

Though this question directly concerns only the theory of poetry, a methodological approach able to find its foundation and justification in a general aesthetic concept and a theory of art is nonetheless required for its solution is. I am, of course, not talking about systematical constructions; a construction can only be a point of departure for aesthetics, a kind of guideline for the consciousness, giving access to objects and helping us to notice and to grasp these objects' authenticity. In order to free the reader as much as possible of complicating thoughts that will only make the subject appear stranger to him, and in order to direct his attention straight towards those points that predetermine the pace and the direction of a real line of inquiry, I will confront him only with some brief remarks of methodological character.

Every science strives to find immediate access to its object, to grasp its data in an undistorted and clear way. At the moment science receives direct access to the source of this knowledge, it obtains a firm basis for all further examinations. However, the discovery of these original data does not represent a similar truth for all science. While in the natural sciences nature gets objectified through its immediate presence into something clear and evident, the question about the first data of social, aesthetic, and juridical phenomena provokes much discord. Here also aesthetics will meet with considerable difficulties. The discord among scholars of aesthetics is to a large extent due to whether they look for and find the origin of aesthetic experience. Therefore in every aesthetic examination the question of the approach towards the immediate data for the aesthetic object should be clearly decided and solved first.

The following sketch flows out of the presupposition (which cannot be explained here in detail) that the first data for aesthetics turn out to be actual aesthetic or artistic experiences (переживание, *Erlebnis*) but in a special sense: neither as a moment nor as a state in the life of the perceiving subject, but as a self-sufficient, closed whole. Here aesthetics differs from psychology: aesthetics is neither interested in the psychological reflection of works of art, nor in challenging psychological reactions, but *in the thingly* (предметную) *foundation* of those subjective impressions that are provided by experience itself. On the other hand, it is clear that this thingly foundation is no manifestation of a physical order. This thingly foundation cannot be identified with the artistic work without reservation in the extent that the thingly foundation is a transcendent-aesthetic experience and exists independently of the artistic work, because what it finds beyond this experience does not have a true aesthetic reality.

This is why the work of art, seen in the way it is understood and examined, for example by art history (that is from the point of view of aesthetics), represents the mere potential that is called into being within the process of aesthetic perception for the first time. Or, what is equally important, the work of art depends on the thingly aesthetic sense of the actual artistic experience.[a] Rhythm is a good example for this. If we look carefully at the character of rhythm in living aesthetic perception, we understand that it cannot be reduced to any (known) lawfulness determining the alternation of the mood of the perceived manifestations; these things are only rhythm's psychic reflection, they are the echo of rhythm but not rhythm itself. In the same way, rhythm does not exhaust itself in the consecution of those sonic vibrations that serve as its physical foundation. However, at the same time rhythm is not identical with meter. This is only an abstract scheme, borrowing its aesthetic sense from the actual perception of rhythms.

II

What are thus the immediately experiential facts of the poetic image? This question cannot be solved through a general examination of artistic images. Rather, it requires a special analysis with regard to the exceptional situation of poetry in comparison to other arts. In other arts, the artistic object itself immediately exists in the aesthetic perception (for example melody, the painted image, the sculpted figure, etc.).

Elements are given to the perceiver through feelings and those elements, which are necessary for the construction, or more precisely, for the reconstruction, of the artistic figure (through the "secondary synthesis" in the terminology of Christiansen).[2] However, this does not apply to poetry, because there the object about which is spoken does not exist. Only the word is immediately given. This primarily symbolical sign is different from the object; it signifies the object by referring to it but not at all by representing it. The object is perceived, grasped and understood through the words. But they are only a medium, a tool for the communication, transmission, and translation of thoughts, of feelings and desires, nothing more. This suggests the following conclusion: If what is given in poetry is not the object itself but only a symbol by which it is signified, and beyond that, signified only incompletely and symbolically, then the object represented by the poet can be reestablished by the perceiver only with the help of the material that the perceiver extracts from authentic experience, but not with the help of that sensory material which is given to the perceiver by the artist – because in poetry this material does not exist.

In this sense, poetry is fundamentally different from all other arts. Contrary to objective painting or the sculpted image, the poetic image has a clearly subjective character, because the listener himself has to undertake the main work in its creation; otherwise the symbols and signs handed out by the poet remain dead and without living aesthetic content. Does this subjectivity of poetic perception not confirm the conviction so widespread in literary criticism that the task of the poet consists solely in the stimulation of the reader's own imagination and that therefore everybody is free to understand and interpret poetic works according to his own taste and inclinations?

The classical theory of poetry, dominant until the end of the 19th century, did not consider these complications. It developed from the assumption that there is a complete correspondence between poetry and representative art. For this theory, the Horazian formula "ut pictura poësis" was an unchallengeable dogma.

At first sight, this analogy really appears as true. Immediate and felt concreteness and intuition are dominant in representative art. To the extent to which poetry strives towards aims like the creation of an artistic image, it must be equated with representative art. Also, poetic speech must be intuitive; that is, it must provoke in the reader or listener concrete, intuitive images. In some way it paints the word: not directly, not naturally, but indirectly, arousing and directing the imagination of the perceiving subject through a special selection of expressions, comparisons, sound-imitation, and other devices.

This conception, which traces its foundation back to Antiquity, determined all further developments of poetry, especially its systematical elaboration in the 18th and 19th centuries. Still Baumgartner defined poetic speech as *oratoria sensitiva perfecta* (perfectly felt speech). Theoretical thinking of Lessing (in the Lakoon) also moved into the same direction, and in Hegel's aesthetics and that of its followers (especially T. F. Fischer), the theory of intuition finally reached philosophical and scientific accomplishment.

The traditional understanding of the poetic image also borders partly on the theory of Potebnia, which distinguishes two kinds of knowledge: the scientific one operating with notions, and the pictorial (образное) one operating with intuitive images. In correspondence with these two, there are also two kinds of speech: the scientific-abstract one and the poetic-pictorial one. Out of this host of ideas grew the romantic idealization of primitive thinking and imagination, which through the pictorial character of childish and primordial (mythological) thinking produced an authentically artistic expression.

However, while the theory of the intuition of poetic speech could appear as a firm and indisputable achievement of scientific and philosophical knowledge until recent times, during the last decade the situation has radically changed. The foundations of this theory began swaying and ask now for radical verification.

The main blow was dealt by the critic T. Meyer[3] who, in his classical examination *Das Stilgesetz der Poesie* (1901), turned the traditional theory of detailed critique inside out. As to its most fundamental points, Meyer's critique can be considered exhaustive. All later examinations of these problems only repeated Meyer's arguments in a more or less modified form without adding anything essential (Dessoir, Cohn, Röteken, et. al.).[4] The objection, however, that has been uttered against Meyer's critical arguments cannot weaken their style and conviction. […]

[What follows is a lengthy presentation of Meyer's work.]

1) If speech is essentially non-figurative, one has to ask: in which way does representation (*Vorstellung*), as it challenges the poetic word, differ from representation as it appears in scientific or practical everyday-speech?

2) Certainly, Meyer points to the fact that, in poetic representation, the word transmits a special actuality (in this sense and in the artistic one) imparting to it an emotional component (*Empfindungsgehalt*) generated by the use of diverse poetic devices (especially that of the choice of words, rhythm, euphonia, sound-imitation, etc.). However, one indication is still missing: emotion can also be an attribute of non-poetic speech. For a satisfying solution of this question it is necessary to show how this emotional component is intimately linked to representations produced by poetic speech, and how it is dependent on the very nature of the artistic word. In Meyer this question remains unanswered. What he considers as most important is the rational (logical) foundation of poetic speech.

This one-sidedness of Meyer's theory partly supplements Christiansen's and his "philosophy of art." In contrast to Meyer's theory, however, Christiansen discovers the full essence of aesthetic perception in the emotional component of art. In his opinion, the work of art is determined in its structure by three fundamental facts: 1) the material out of which it is made (for example marble, color, sound, words); 2) the thing (предмет) of its content (i.e. that which it represents); 3) the form in the largest sense of the word, that is the entirety of the means and devices of the expression, partly grounded in the material itself (which explains the formal beauty independent of the thingly-sensory content). These factors are so different in nature that one cannot simply by combining them, create the kind of unity of artistic impression which is characteristic for the aesthetic object. Therefore this unity must be rooted in something else. According to Christiansen, this other element is the emotional side of artistic experience. Each of these elements, as it enters the "mixture" that is the work of art, has its own fundamental emotional tone (тон), i.e. the perception is accompanied by something that is *emotionally stimulated*. This is not the autonomous entirety of feeling and mood, but only its constitutive parts, elementary and "differential." These elements, by flowing together, create aesthetic experience as a whole. Christiansen calls this elementary stimulation *"Stimmungsimpressionen"* (emotional impressions). They accompany the work of art just as much as the single elements, and thus also have a composed character (for example color or sound or their combinations), no matter if these elements belong to the formal side of the work, to its material or to the subject of sensible content.

Like this, the character of emotional impressions is completely dependent on the nature of those elements to which they are linked. Not only do different elements belong to the same order (as for example sound and color), but elements of different orders (for example the sensible and the formal) can also arouse similar and even identical impressions. The unity of the work of art (its style) is therefore dependent on the fact that all elements and emotional factors by which the work of art is formed are in agreement with each other; that is to say that they have one unique emotional tone.

From there it becomes clear that in aesthetic perception the main meaning is not on the intuitively felt side of the work: this side is only a point of departure. The aesthetic object in its proper sense is constructed out of those emotional, formless (безобразный) expressions which the work of art arouses in the subject by its sensitive material; and to the same extent the aesthetic object is deprived of any form. Poetry is in this regard no exception. In poetry the formlessness of the aesthetic object becomes even particularly clear. The intuitive image, challenging our consciousness with poetic speech, is non-essential. All essence in the accompanying perception of the speech is represented by formless emotional impressions. This explains, for example, the artistic meaning; by modifying (сопрягать, conjugate) the uni-tonal form, the artist heightens the intensity of the emotional impression.

Christiansen's theory offers refinement as well as a considerable depth of artistic analysis. However, the solutions he suggests to our problems cannot fully satisfy us and suffer from essential phenomenological shortcomings.

Evaluating emotional impressions as the aesthetic foundation of artistic perception, Christiansen's reflections do not lead to a clear distinction between those emotional moments which are known by a corresponding subject (*my* feeling, arising under the influence or through the impulse of the work's data), and those which are perceived as characteristics of the object itself (the one which interests the theory of empathy. Among them, only the latter are essential for the structure of the aesthetic object. But only these are *grounded* in the thingly image, and they form with it one inseparable, primordial unity. Thus, if, as Christiansen suggests, the essence of the aesthetic object is determined only by emotional impressions and these impressions are qualitatively (not essentially) independent of the objective facts by which they are provoked, the thingly side of the object appears as indifferent. In this case, the aesthetic object will be degraded to not more than a cause for the stimulation of these or other feelings or emotional impressions. This underestimation of the thingly side of the aesthetic object conceals in itself serious dangers for aesthetics. Irrespective of the fact that it will finally join romantic aesthetic tendencies that were rejected even by Christiansen, it threatens to turn aesthetic evaluation into something entirely unthingly and illusory, leaving it exposed to arbitrary subjectivism.

While the traditional theory of intuition forces itself to interpret poetry analogous to the representative arts, Christiansen goes in the opposite direction: he attributes something non-formal (безобразность) that is characteristic for the poetic word, to other arts as well.

But in principle, this does not change anything, nor does it provide any benefit for the theory of poetry, because in the one or the other case poetry is introduced into a general scheme through which it gets equated with other arts. Here the particularities of the poetic word and its aesthetic potential remain undiscovered. In other words, Lessing's mentioned highest methodological principle remains unused.

For these reasons we must once again ask the same questions: what is the meaning of intuition and form (образность) in poetry? How can they be phenomonologically described, and, if possible, explained and justified? […]

Note by the author

a. Art historians often forget what the work of art is. The work of art represents for them only an object of research, like the phenomenon of nature in natural sciences. This is why in its research just the most essential facts receive no attention.

Notes by the translator

1.   Source: "О природе поэтического образа" in *Lietuvos universiteto humanitariniu mokslu fakulteto rastai,* book 1 (Kaunas: 1925), pp. 423–481.

2.   For Broder Christiansen see Chapter 1, note 23.

3.   Theodor A. Meyer: *Das Stilgezetz der Poesie* (Darmstadt: Wissenschaftliche Buchgesellschaft, 1901. A new edition has been published by Suhrkamp (Frankfurt) in 1990 with a preface by Wolfgang Iser.

4.   Max Dessoir (1867–1947): "Anschauung und Bescheibung" in *Archiv für systematische Philosophie* 10, 1904, pp. 20–65. Jonas Cohn (1869–1947): "Die Anschaulichkeit der dichterischen Sprache" in *Zeitschrift für Aesthetik* 2, 1907, pp. 182–201.

Appendix III

The Foundations of Politics (1927)

Lev Platonovich Karsavin

I

If we want to characterize the systematic study of culture as a whole, we choose the old Aristotelian term 'politika' (stately entirety). The prevailing antithesis of society and state is here sublated, and together with this, the state adopts the quality of a clearly determined unity and the wholeness of a cultural organism. When studying culture by looking at its entirety or constitutive principle, we reject the notion of culture as a simply systematically unified "independent" sphere (state, social structure, economic structure, spiritual culture). We also reject the monistic understanding of culture – it is impossible to understand the whole state based on the attributes of one of its parts (for example "the economical sphere"). Also, we reject the disregard of the most essential principle of culture, the principle of its unity, which does not overlap with one part of the sphere (though it participates with one of them, namely with that of the state).

All this represents a decisive break with sociology, which has claimed until now – without success – the title of a science, and becomes more and more helplessly muddled in approximate generalizations and primitive attempts to determine its "method." Sociology turns out to be a characteristic product of the European rationalist-individualist development. And not by coincidence has materialist Marxism occurred as the best and most powerful sociology because it is theoretically (not in practice) negating the state, that is, negating the living and spiritual-personal unity of culture.

We Russians find ourselves in an exceptionally good situation. We had our "Europe" with the face of the pre-Revolutionary social class. And this "Russian Europe" overtook its motherland, the "European Europe," fearlessly drew the ultimate conclusions from the premise of European culture, and actively anticipated the threat of Europe's deadly crisis.

However, with the fall of the "Russian Europe" the Eurasian Russia is born, opening itself like a huge world-culture, like a new *Weltanschauung*. Soon old forms and old terms become inadequate: in the new forms becomes manifest the eternal essence of all cultures. It is not through minor repairs, through naïve name-changes as it is done by sociologists and "social science," that the problem will be solved, but rather through a new *weltanschauliche* device. What replaces sociology in the new cultural epoch is "politics."

Politics is constructed neither on individual-materialist nor on idle relativistic assumptions and hypotheses, but on philosophical scholarship and personality. Scholarship clarifies the nature and the construction of the subject of culture that is the personality of the *sobor* (communality) and the nature of the state; it clarifies the forms determining the personal being of the subject and the organization of culture; it clarifies the sense of the spiritual and the material expression of the culture-subject; and it clarifies the relation between the culture-subject and its accomplishment, for example religio-moral activities and the sense of truth.

In the present article I suggest only a basic sketch of politics; at first sight this sketch does not look very systematical and leaves even some important problems untouched. For example, it does not mention the problems of historiosophy. It mentions only problems of spiritual and material culture but does not provide a critique of the modern, individual-istic *Weltanschauung*. Nor do I speak exhaustively of the problem of re-ligion. However, I must confine myself to the limited space provided and deal with ideas of several authors who are working on the subject of Eura-sia. And in spite of this the general foundation of the system seems to ap-pear with sufficient clearness. More we do not require here.

II

The meaning of existence becomes clear though certain cultural values, which the subject constantly keeps and modifies. These values form an organic unity that we call culture. Culture is not the simple sum of values and still less their system, but an organic unity, always presupposing the existence of some subjects, who create, conserve, and develop these val-ues. Only within these values can culture exist.

Living culture always has the capacity to develop and to perfection-ate itself. In each of its "moments" resides its particularity, unrepeatable and irreplaceable, unique and necessary for the existence of culture as a whole. However, solely from the point of view of the whole culture, there are more and less valuable moments and periods. In this way, all moments of culture possess an "original equality" and a "co-relative inequality" (or a "hierarchical co-relationship"). From this arise contradictions which must inevitably be dealt with empirically, but only can be entirely over-come by metaphysics and religion.

Culture is produced by the *free subject* and it is a free manifestation of itself, partly living and partly settled, partly derived from the subject and hardened in the form of a *tradition* which the subject freely accepts, tolerates, or modifies in correspondence with the "soul" or the values of culture, or, in the very end, in correspondence with himself. It is therefore necessary, in culture, to distinguish between historical tradition and the present on the one hand, and future or the sphere of freely set aims on the other. Still, because the aims are set by the cultural subject itself [by the artist, writer, etc., T. B-B.], these aims are determined by the subject's characteristics, and by this they are in accordance with the historical tradition. In this way, the *unity* of culture and the freedom of its subject are preserved, because when moments of culture spread out over time and space, their subject is not restricted to *its own* time and space, but contains time and space in itself and exists beyond them.

Culture as a whole and limited entity has priority in its single manifestations and moments, from which stems the respect for tradition in the very act of creation of the new, and the justification of this act in the conservation of the tradition. In the single part, culture has priority, as much as in the outer expressions of its unity and its organization, i.e. in the state. The subject develops perhaps individually or communally (symphonically). The notion of "culture" is almost always used for subjects of the second kind. One speaks of the "cultural man," assuming that his special quality is his culture, and one speaks of the culture of mankind, of a people, of a social class. But "class," "people," "mankind," are also examples of communal subjects. The symphonic subject is not the agglomeration or simple sum of individual subjects, but its congruence (согласование), uniting multiplicity and individuality into the highest form of All-Unity. Therefore, the nation is not the sum of social groups (social classes for example), but their organic and harmonious hierarchic unity. The culture of a people is not the sum but the symphonic unity of more partial cultures, and it does not exist otherwise than as their real, concrete unity and at the same time beyond them. In this way, ethnic cultures (народние культуры) can form a large cultural unity (Hellenic, European, Eurasian), which takes the existence of a special communal subject for granted. However much we talk of the culture of mankind, we do not think of it as an abstract unity but as something which concerns multi-ethnic and ethnic cultures, and not just one of them, but their real concrete unity as it is spread over time and space.

From this it follows that one can create a general human culture only by creating its national and multi-national parts, and that the event of a corresponding cultural circle will at times dominate the decisive meaning for all cultural development of mankind. The Russian Revolution is such an event through which Russia-Eurasia manifests its *general-human* thought and reveals itself as the *historical mission of Russia*. The fate of Asian culture is also linked to the fate of Russia. Therefore Asia is just about to recognize its own being in a new fashion. Equally linked to Russian culture is the exit of European culture from its persisting individualistic crisis. Exit or death.

III

The communal or symphonic subject is not less real than the individual but even more real. The individual seen in the light, in which it normally presents itself, simply does not exist. It is an invention or a fiction. Man is "individual" not because he is free and separated from the others and the whole, or is able to isolate himself, but because he for himself specifically expresses and materializes through himself and through his particularity the whole, that is, the highest *supra-individual* consciousness and the highest supra individual will. Other "individuals" express and materialize the same things, but in another fashion. Everybody expresses this consciousness for himself and "individually," but on the whole, all individuals are non-separated. If this Highest did not exist, the individual could express nothing solely for itself and therefore could not materialize itself. It simply could not exist. On the other hand, the richer the content of this "highest" is, the richer also is the fully individual existence. *But outside its "individual" manifestation, outside the community of free individuals, and in a way other than freely and united, the "highest" does not exist.* Therefore one should not understand the "highest" as an abstraction from the individual, as something that would constrain its freedom and predetermine its action. The "highest" materializes itself in the free acts of every individual. It is the aforementioned unity of all individuality, entering into the unity and expressing it; and at the same time it is the multitude of individuals. The "communal" neither denies nor limits the individual in a way in which the "collective" does. By "collective" I mean the "assembled" (sbornoe) or "gathered" (sobrannoe). *For the being of the communal whole the expression of its multitude is essential, that is to say the sphere of individual being as the expression of unity, or the natural correspondence of individuals.* It is a unity, but not simply for itself, *but as a unity it expresses itself unavoidably through a multitude.* And both the multitude and the individual function *as partial centers of specific expressions of the whole.* The unity of individuals is not at all the impersonal sphere of values and not a metaphysical subject. So, how can the individual express it *personally*, and how can it be a personality? This unity is, not more and not less than the individual, a *personality*, but it materializes itself *only* personally in a free individual personality.

However, one also needs to consider that no empirical reality and no empirical subject will ever be accomplished. Empirically, not one sin-

gle communal subject attains the full degree of its unity, but remains only
on its way there. It remains "harmonious" or "symphonic" and thus not
accomplished. I do not want to say that this state of harmony is useless
and not an absolute value. It is necessary as a movement towards the formation and existence of the symphonic subject, which, in spite of this, is
absolutely unique, and absolutely multiple. Abstract universalism tried not
to recognize this empirical multitude, tried not to recognize individualism
as the only reality, and tried not to postulate the whole empirical unity on
the basis of a multitude. In the case of abstract universalism, the specificity and reality of the empirical were negated. However, empirical elements
should be negated only in the sense that they are not the whole existence
of the symphonic subject; they signify *only a moment* of this existence,
and, in addition to this, an unaccomplished moment. The empirical community subject "forgets" about its unity, about its multitude. Empirical
Being is linked to struggle and violence. The individual exaggerates its
meaning as a "singular," it separates itself from the others and from the
whole and tries to see itself as a self-contained aim. Sometimes it negates
the whole and sometimes it believes that only its "singularity" is the expression of the whole. This mirage appears as the result of the negation of
the whole, and as a result of forgetting about the whole or as a "lie" (because truth is "remembering").

All this is even more obvious because our "self-consciousness," our
'I', can in no case be compared with some clearly traced sphere. Most
probably the 'I' is similar to a center that sometimes coincides with a
mathematical point and sometimes expands itself and transforms into a
sphere with several radii dependent on the circumference of individualization.

So, sometimes the 'I' signifies the sphere of narrow egoistic interests opposing the 'Other.' Sometimes it signifies the self-consciousness of
social groups when man appropriates those groups' will and ideology
though, it is true, he always appropriates these wills' individualization (for
example in acts of thought). Sometimes the 'I' signifies the consciousness
of the whole of mankind, though this happens also through individualization. However, in reality, the 'I' as it expresses the whole, expresses its
self-identical-individual, and because it is the bearer of a *cantus firmus*, it
provokes the polyphony of existence.

In this originally built personality resides the secret of personal
Being. In it is found the mystery of creative life acts, for example self-
renunciation (it is always the smaller or lower part of my 'I' that I sacrifice
in order to obtain the higher part of my 'I'). Finally, it also reflects the
whole structure of society. In the unaccomplished empirical reality, the
individual unavoidably strives towards the lower sphere of its 'I'. It

attempts to lock itself into the sphere of its egoistic interests, negating other individual spheres and wholes, and attempting to absorb and transform all the rest. When the individuum or something exterior is submitted to the limits of individual-egoistic interests, the individual destroys the whole, and by annihilating other individuals, it also annihilates itself. (We can observe the opposite example in collectivism, which, through the highest spheres of unity of the individual "evaporates" the individuals, and transforms, in this way, this unity of individuals into impersonality and abstraction. And by destroying the individual sphere the collective sphere finally destroys itself). So what is it that really protects and conserves individual being? We should not answer this question by defining this "what" as an absolutely impenetrable sphere. Rather we should trace the limits of its egoistic expressions.

The whole does not exist abstractly, in itself, but *only through the individual, in individuals, and in the quality of the contemporary and all-encompassing unity of individuals, a unity which also manifests itself as the "moments" of the individuals, each of which expresses itself.* Therefore, *when the whole exists, the expression of its multiple individuals also exists. Every single one of those individuals exists as the freest realization of itself within the specific sphere of the whole.* In this way, the whole is not the sum of all individual spheres, nor is it impenetrable for individuals. This is because: if those individuals did not appear as a whole, the whole itself could not exist. In the same way, outside the individual sphere there is no separate sphere of the whole. This sphere exists in the real unity and the (only empirical) real overlapping of the multitude of the individual sphere with the whole.

At the same time, this understanding differs from pure individualism and from collectivism because the latter recognizes only the all-encompassing sphere of an abstract whole, and the former only recognizes the individual sphere. […]

Note

1. Source: "Основы политики" in *Evraziiskii Vremennik* 5 (Berlin: 1927) extracts.

A Letter by Henri Parland from Kaunas[1]

Kovno 3.VI.29

Liebe Mama

Aus meinen Stellen in Finnland ist jetzt nichts zu hören gewesen, also bleibe ich vorläufig noch hier. Bis zum Zehnten bleibe ich in meinem jetzigen Zimmer, dann ziehe ich in Onkel Tuttis um. Onkel Tutti wird wohl dann schon seine Reise nach Russland angetreten haben.

Ich bin ganz gesund, bin stark eingebrannt und fühle mich ausgezeichnet. Ich arbeite immer weiter an meinen Artikeln, heute Abend beendige ich wohl wieder einen. Auf Französisch las ich Stendhal und Gide, der erstgenannte ist nur furchtbar kompliziert durch seine unendlich langen Sätze.

Es ist unterdessen kalt und regnerisch geworden. D.h. es regnet jede halbe Stunde und gleich nach dem Regen wird es kalt. Wir haben daher in den letzten Tagen nicht gebadet und sind überhaupt wenig draußen gewesen.

Freitag führte mich Onkel Tutti in die Oper: Traviata. Ich habe sie früher noch nie gehört und die Rollen wurden von Sängern aus Moskau gesungen. Es war sehr schön.

Ich habe einen ausgezeichneten neuen Aufschlag für einen Artikel bekommen: hier in Kovno gibt es ein jüdisches Theater das direkt vom berühmten Moskauer jüdischen Theater ausgeht und überhaupt das einzige in Westeuropa ist. Ich war neulich auf einer Vorstellung, eine Dame, die an diesem Theater arbeitet (diejenige, die mir französische Stunden gibt) führte mich hin. Ich muss sagen: nie habe ich im Theater etwas so wirkungsvolles gesehen. Ich werde nächstens versuchen, darüber zu schreiben. […]

Jedenfalls: eben steht ja alles ausgezeichnet. Alle Menschen sind freundlich und liebenswürdig gegen mich, Onkel Tuttis Wirte sind sehr nette, gute Leute. Sie haben einen Sohn, der eben das Studentenexamen macht und sich auf Literatur etc. versteht, ich glaube mehr als ich es tue. Onkel Tuttis Buch ist endlich herausgekommen, er hat mit ihm sehr viel Mühe gehabt. […]

[…] bei Onkel Tutti war Professor Karsavin, ein wirklich interessanter Mensch. Ich weiß nicht, ob ich Euch schon geschrieben habe, dass ich auf seiner (leider) letzten Vorlesung in der Universität war, es war et-

was ganz anderes als gewöhnliche Vorlesungen. Also auf Wiedersehen,
grüß die Brüder und Pappi.

Note

1.   The Finland-Swedish poet Henri Parland (1908–1930) was the son of Sesemann's sister
Ida Maria and was born, like Sesemann, in Vyborg. Though he died at the age of 22 of scarlet
fever, he is credited with introducing formalism and semiotics into Finland. In 1929, his parents
– worried about his bohemian Helsinki lifestyle – sent him to his uncle in Kaunas (Kovno) from
where Henri wrote poems and literature but also pieces about newly discovered phenomena such
as "Baltic jazz." Henri lived in Sesemann's apartment and refers in his letters to Sesemann as
"Onkel Tutti." He spoke German with his mother (which explains why the present letter is in
German) but generally wrote in Swedish. For further reading see Stam 1998 and Parland 1991.

Appendix V:

Bibliography of Vasily Sesemann's Works

1. Works in Languages other than Lithuanian (in Chronological Order)

"Рациональное и иррациональное в системе философии" in *Logos* 2 (Moscow: 1911), 93–122. German version in the parallel German issue of *Logos* 2 (Tübingen: 1911), 208–242: "Das Rationale und das Irrationale im System der Philosophie."

"Die Ethik Platos und das Problem des Bösen" in *Sammelband H. Cohen zum 70. Geburtstag* (1912), 170–189.

"Der Rhythmos und seine Bedeutung für Erziehung und Kunst. Ein Beitrag zur Würdigung der Rhythmischen Gymnastik" (St. Petersburg: Bericht der St. Katharinen Schule, 1913), 3–37.

"Теорическая философия марбургской школы" in Новые идеи в философии (St. Petersburg: 1913), 1–34.

"Линвистические спектры г. Морозова и платоновский вопрос" in *Известия отделения пусссково языка и словесности российской академий наук*, Nr. 22 (Petrograd 1917): 70–80.

"Эстетическая одецка историй искусства" in *Мысль* Nr. 1, 1922.

"Обозрение новейшей германской философиской литературы" in *София: проблемы духовной культуры и религиозной философии* (Berlin: 1923), 173–183.

"Das Problem des Idealismus in der Philosophie" in *Lietuvos universiteto humanitariniu mokslu fakulteto rastai*, book 1 (Kaunas: 1925), 103–121.

"О природе поэтического образа" in *Lietuvos universiteto humanitariniu mokslu fakulteto rastai,* book 1 (Kaunas: 1925), 423–481.

"Сократ и проблема самопознания" in *Евразийский временник* (Berlin: 1925), Book 4, 224–267.

"Платонизм, Плотин и современность" in *Logos 1,* (Prague, 1925), 229–235.

"Nikolai Hartmann, Grundzüge einer Metaphysik der Erkenntnis" [review] in *Logos* (Prague: 1925), book 1, 229–235.

"Beiträge zum Erkenntnisproblem I: Über gegenständliches und ungegenständliches Wissen" in *Lietuvos universiteto Humanitariniu mokslu fakulteto rastai* (Kaunas: 1927): 69–142.

"Beiträge zum Erkenntnisproblem II: Rationales und Irrationales" in *Lietuvos uiversiteto Humanitariniu mokslu fakulteto rastai*, vol. 3:4 (Kaunas: 1927): 127–192.

"Zum Problem des reinen Wissens" Sonderabdruck aus *Philosophischer Anzeiger* Jahrgang 2. Heft 2: 204–235, Heft 3: 324–344 (Bonn: 1927)

"Искусство и культура: к проблеме эстетики" in *Версты* 2 (Paris: 1927): 185–204.

"Martin Heidegger: Sein und Zeit" [review] in *Путь* 14 (Paris: 1928): 117–123.

"Beiträge zum Erkenntnisproblem III: Das Logisch Rationale" in *Eranus* Nr 1 (Kaunas: 1930): 129–195.

"Logik und Ontologie der Möglichkeit: August Faust. Der Möglichkeits-gedanke. 1. Teil: Antike Philosophie. 2. Teil: Chistliche Phi-losophie" in *Blätter für deutsche Philosophie* Bd. 10, Heft 2 (Heidelberg: 1932): 161–171.

"Die bolschewistische Philosophie in Sowiet Russland" in *Der russische Gedanke* Heft 2 (Bonn: 1931): 176–183.

"Die logischen Gesetze und das Sein: a) Die logischen Gesetze im Verhältnis zum subjektbezogenen und psychischen Sein. b) Die logischen Gesetze und das daseinsautonome Sein" in *Eranus* Vol 2 (Kaunas: 1931): 60–230.

"Zum Problem der logischen Paradoxien" in *Eranus* vol. 3 (Kaunas: 1935): 5–85.

"Zum Problem der Dialektik" in *Blätter für deutsche Philosophie* Bd. 9, Heft 1 (Berlin: 1935): 28–61.

"Introduction" (in Russian) to Alexandr Veideman's book *Предмед Познания: Основная Часть (Мышление и Бытие)* (Riga: Sfinkss, 1937): iv–x.

"Пустые и универсальные классы в современной символической логике" in *Lietuvos TSR aukstuju mokyklu mokslo darbai. Filosofija* Vol. II: 2 (Vilnius: 1962): 31–63.

Философиа религии [manuscript] (University of Vilnius, Library)

Критические замечания к 'очерку диалектического материализма' typescript] 1949, 5 p. (University of Vilnius, Central Archive)

Логика [typescript], 95 p. (University of Vilnius, Library)

К проблеме познания [manuscript], 37 p. (University of Vilnius, library)

Закон тождества в формльной и диалектической логике [manu-script], 49 p. (University of Vilnius, Library)

2. Works in Lithuanian

Logika (Kaunas: Lietuvos universitetuo Humanitariniu mokslu fakultete, 1929), 304 p.

Paskaitos (Lectures) (Kaunas: Humanitariniu mokslu fakultetas, 1929)

Estetika (Vilnius: Mintis, 1970), 463 p.
The Lithuanian edition of Sesemann's works consists of two volumes of
    Works (=Rastai)
Vol. 1: *Gnoseologia* (Vilnius: Mintis, 1987)
Vol. 2: *Filosofijos istorija* (Vilnius: Mintis, 1997)

3. Translations by Sesemann

Lossky's *Logica* (Petrograd: Nauka i shkola, 2 vol. 1922) as *Handbuch
    der Logik* (Leipzig: Teubner, 1927), 445 pages.
Aristotle's *De Anima* as: *Aristotelis: Apie siela* (Vilnius: Valstybini poli-
    tiais ir mokslinis literatûros leidykla, 1959) with a 60 pages
    long introduction into the philosophy of Aristotle.

Bibliography

Bakhtin, Mikhail. 1975. "Problema soderzhanija, materiala i forma v slovesnom tvorchestve" in *Voprosy literatury i estetiki*. Moscow: Khudozh. literatura.
———. 1990. *Art and Answerability*. Austin: University of Texas Press.
Berdaev, N.A. "Iz etiudov o ya Beme: etiud 1. Uchenie ob ungrunde i svobodie" [Studies Concerning Jacob Böhme Etude I: The Teaching about the Ungrund and Freedom] in *Put'* 1930: 20, pp. 47–79.
Bergson, Henri. 1922. *Durée et simultanéité: A propos de la théorie d'Einstein*. Paris: Alcan.
———. *La Penseé et le mouvant*. 1987. Paris: Quadrige [1934].
———. *L'Energie spirituelle: essais et conférences*. 1919. Paris: Alcan.
———. *L'Ideé de lieu chez Aristote* in Mélanges. 1972. Paris: Presses universitaires de France [Alcan, 1889].
———. *Matière et mémoire*. 1997. Paris: Presses universitaires de France [1896].
Besrodny, C. H. 1992. "Zur Geschichte des Russischen Neukantianismus: Die Zeitschrift "Logos" und ihre Redakteure," *Zeitschrift für Slavistik* 37/ 4, pp. 489–511.
Binswanger, Ludwig. 1953. *Grundformen und Erkenntnis des menschlichen Daseins*. Zürich: Niehans.
Bréhier, Emile. 1968. *Histoire de la philosophie* t. II, 4; 19e Siècle après 1850 – Le 20e Siècle. Paris: Presses universitaires de France.
Broms, Henri. 1985. *Alkukuvien jäljillä- Kulttuurin semiotiikkaa*. Juva: WSOY.
Cohen, Hermann. 1912. *Ästhetik des reinen Gefühls*, 2 Bd. Berlin: Cassirer, Bd. II.
———. 1977. *Logik der reinen Erkenntnis* (1914) *Werke* 6. Hildesheim: George Olms.
Curtis, James H. 1976. "Bergson and Russian Formalism" in *Comparative Literature* 28 Spring.
Deleuze, Gilles. 1966. *Le Bergsonisme*. Paris: Presses universitaires de France.
Devereux, George. 1976. *Dreams in Greek Tragedy*. Berkeley & Los Angeles; University of California Press.
Edie, James, James Scanlan, Mary-Barbara Zeldin (eds). 1976. *Russian Philosophy* (Vol. III). Knoxville: University of Tennessee Press.
Fink, Hilary L. 1999. *Bergson and Russian Hodernism 1900–1930*. Evanston: Northwestern University Press.

Fizer, John. 1986. *Alexander A. Potebnja's Psycho-Linguistic Theory of Literature: A Metacritical Inquiry.* Cambridge: Harvard Ukrainian Research Institute.

Florenskii, Pavel A. 1990. *Stolp i utverzhdenie istiny.* Moscow: Izdatel'stvo Pravda, 2 Vols.

———. 1997. *The Pillar and Ground of the Truth.* Princeton, NJ: Princeton UP.

Gessen, Sergei I. 1909. *Individuelle Kausalität:* Studien zum transzendentalen Empirismus. Berlin: Reuther & Reinhardt.

———. 1910. "Mistika i metafisika" *Logos* 1 (Moscow), pp. 92–112.

———. 1916. "Novyi opyt intuitivnoi filosofii," *Severnie Zapiski* (April-May), pp. 222–37.

Greimas, Algirdas Julien. 1966. *Sémantique structurale.* Paris: Larousse.

———. 1973. "Toward a Theory of Modalities" in: *On Meaning: Selected Writings in Semiotic Theory.* Minneapolis: University of Minnesota Press.

Gurvitch, Georges. 1928. "La philosophie russe du premier quart du XXe siècle" in *Le Monde slave* 8.

Hartmann, Nicolai. 1958. "Buchbesprechung zu Wilhelm Sesemann" in *Kantstudien* 1931, 227–232, reprinted in *Kleinere Schriften.* Berlin: De Gruyter. Bd. 2: 368–374.

———. 1957. "Zeitlichkeit und Substanzialität" in *Kleinere Schriften I.* Berlin: De Gruyter.

———. 1966. *Möglichkeit und Wirklichkeit.* Berlin: De Gruyter.

———. 1924. "Diesseits von Idealismus und Realismus" *Kantstudien* 29, pp. 160–206.

Heidegger, Martin. 1959. *Unterwegs zur Sprache.* Frankfurt: Klostermann.

Hufen, Christian. 2001. *Fedor Stepun: Ein politischer Intellectueller aus Russland und Europa: Die Jahre 1884–1945.* Berlin: Lukas.

Humboldt, Wilhelm von. 1974. *Über die Verschiedenheit des menschlichen Sprachbaues und ihren Einfluß auf die geistige Entwicklung des Menschengeschlechts* Hildesheim & New York: Olms [1880].

———. 1836–39. *Über die Kawi-Sprache auf der Insel Jawa: Nebst einer Einleitung über die Verschiedenheit des menschlichen Sprachbausund ihren Einfluß auf die geistige Entwicklung des Menschengeschlechts.* Berlin: Königl. Akademie der Wissenschaften. Russian trans.: *Orazlichii organizmov chelovecheskovo jazika i o vlijanii etovo razlichiya na ymstvennoyo razvitie chelovecheskovo roda (posmertnoe sochinenie Vilgelma fon Gumbolta).* St. Petersburg: Imperial Academy of Sciences, 1859.

James, William. 1902. *The Varieties of Religious Experience*. London: Longmans.

Jankélévitch, Vladimir. *Henri Bergson*. 1959. Paris: Presses universitaires de France

―――. 1974. *L'Irréversible et la nostalgie*. Paris: Flammarion.

Kimura, Bin. 1982. 時間と自己 (Jikan to jiko; Time and I). Tokyo: Iwanami.

―――. 1991. "Signification et limite dans la formation psychothérapeutique" in Fedida, P. and Schotte, J. (eds). *Psychiatrie et existence*. Grenoble: Millon, 1991.

―――. 1992. *Ecrits de psychopathologie phénoménologique*. Paris; Presses Universitaires francaises.

Kohn, Hans. 1953. *Pan-Slavism: Its History and Ideology*. Notre Dame: Notre Dame University Press.

Kotorova, E. 1997. "Ponjatie 'vnutrennei formy' v rossiiskom i sovetskom iazykoznanii" in *Romantic-Germanic Linguistic Investigations and the Methods of Language Teaching. Proceedings of an International Conference*. Tomsk: Pedagogical University, pp. 18–22.

Lacan, Jacques. 1973. *Les quatre concepts fondamentaux de la psychanalyse: Le séminaire, Livre XI*, 1964. Paris: Seuil.

―――. *De la psychose paranoïaque dans ses rapports avec la personnalité*. Paris:, 1975.

Lipps, Theodor. 1902. *Von der ästhetischen Apperzeption*, Halle: Niemeyer.

Lossky, Nicolas O. 1991. *Istoriia russkoi filosofii*. Moscow: Vysshaia shkola.

―――. 1928. *The World as an Organical Whole*. Oxford: Oxford University Press.

―――. 1926. "Fichtes konkrete Ethik im Lichte des modernen Transcendentalismus" in *Logos* 15, pp. 349–63.

―――. 1914. *Intuitivnaja filosofija Bergsona*. Moscow.

Marti, Jean. 1976. "La psychanalyse russe" in *Critique* 346.

Medvedev, Pavel N. 1928. *Formalistyi v literaturoprovedenii*. Leningrad: Priboi. Engl. trans: *The Formal Method Literary Scholarship*, Cambridge MA, Harvard University Press, 1985.

Nemeth, Thomas. 1998. "The Rise of Neo-Kantianism: Vvedensky's Early Critical Philosophy" in *Studies in East European Thought* 50: pp. 119–151.

―――. 1999. "From Neo-Kantianism to Logicism: Vvedensky's Mature Years," *Studies in East European Thought* 51, pp. 1–33.

————. 1998. "Russian Neo-Kantianism." *The Routledge Encyclopedia of Philosophy.* Ed. E. Craig. London and NY: Routledge, pp. 792–797.

Nethercott, Frances. 1995. *Une Rencontre philosophique: Bergson en Russie* (1907–1917). Paris: Harmattan.

Parland, Oscar. 1991. *Kunskap och inlevelse* [Knowledge and Empathy]. Esbo: Schildt.

Potebnia, Aleksandr. 1999. *Mysl' i iazyk.* Moscow: Labirint [1862].

Rickert, Heinrich. 1902. *Die Grenzen der naturwissenschaftlichen Begriffsbildung: Eine logische Einleitung in die historischen Wissenschaften.* Tübingen: Mohr.

Roudinesco, Elisabeth. 1990. *J. Lacan & Co.* Chicago: Chicago University Press.

Rudova, Larissa. 1996. "Bergsonism in Russia: The Case of Bakhtin" in *Neophilologus* 80, pp. 175–188.

Ruskino, Elaine. 1982. "Acmeism, Post-Symbolism and Henri Bergson" in *Slavic Rewiev* 41.

Scheler, Max. 1973. *Selected Philosophical Essays.* Evanston IL: Northwestern University Press.

————. 1976. *Späte Schriften.* Bern: Francke.

Scherrer, Jutta. 1974. "Les societés 'philosophico-religieuses' et la quête idéologique de l'intelligentsia russe avant 1917," *Cahiers du monde russe et soviétique* XV: 3–4, juillet-dec., pp. 297–314.

Schlögel, K. et al., (eds). 1999. *Chronik Russischen Lebens in Deutschland 1918–1941.* Berlin: Akademie Verlag.

Schleiermacher, Friedrich. 1958. *Über die Religion: Reden an die Gebildeten unter ihren Verachtern* [1799]. Hamburg: Meiner.

Schweizer, Robert. 1993. *Die Wiborger Deutschen.* Helsinki: Veröffentlichungen der Stiftung zur Förderung deutscher Kultur.

Sharf, Robert H. "Experience." 1998. In Mark. C. Taylor (ed.), *Critical Terms for Religious Studies.* Chicago: University of Chicago Press.

Sesemann, Vaslily. 1911. "Razional'noe i irrazional'noe v sisteme filosofii" in *Logos* (Moscow), pp. 93–122.

————. "'Lingvicheskie spektry' g. Morozova i Platonskii vopros." Petrograd: Izvestiia Otdeleniia Russkogo iazyka i slovestnosti Rossiiskoi Akademii Nauk, 1917.

————. 1925. "Nikolai Hartmann, Grundzüge einer Metaphysik der Erkenntnis" [review] in *Logos* (Prague), book 1: pp. 229–35.

———. 1927a. "Beiträge zum Erkenntnisproblem I: Über gegenständliches und ungegenständliches Wissen" in *Lietuvos universiteto Humanitariniu mokslu fakulteto rastai* (Kaunas), pp. 69–142.

———. 1927b. "Beiträge zum Erkenntnisproblem II: Rationales und Irrationales" in *Lietuvos universiteto Humanitariniu mokslu fakulteto rastai*, vol. 3:4 (Kaunas), pp. 127–92.

———. 1927c. "Iskusstvo i kul'tura (k probleme estetiki)," *Versty* (Paris) 2, pp. 185–204.

———. 1928. "Martin Heidegger: Sein und Zeit" [review]. *Put'* 14 (Paris), pp. 117–23.

———. 1929a. *Logika.* Kaunas: Lietuvos universitetuo Humanitariniu mokslu fakultete.

———. 1929b. *Paskaitos* (Lectures). Kaunas: Humanitariniu mokslu fakultetas.

———. 1930. "Beiträge zum Erkenntnisproblem III: Das Logisch Rationale," *Eranus* 1 (Kaunas), pp. 129–195.

———. 1931. "Die logischen Gesetze und das Sein: a) Die logischen Gesetze im Verhältnis zum subjekt-bezogenen und psychischen Sein. b) Die logischen Gesetze und das daseinsautonome Sein," *Eranus* 2 (Kaunas), pp. 60–230.

1935a. *Estetika: Musu laiku gnoseologijai naujai besiorientuojant.* Eranus (Kaunas)

———. 1935b. *Zum Problem der logischen Paradoxien.* Eranus 3 (Kaunas), p. 5–85.

———. 1970. *Estetika.* Vilnius: Mintis.

———. 1987. *Works* (=Rastai) Vol. 1: *Gnoseologia* (Vilnius: Mintis, 1987); Vol. 2: *Filosofijos istorija.* Vilnius: Mintis.

Shklovsky, 1923. Vicotor. *Literatura i kinematograf.* Berlin.

Shpet, Gustav. 1991. *Appearance and Sense: Phenomenology as the Fundamental Sciece and Its Problems.* Trans. T. Nemeth. *Phaenomenologica* 120. Dordrecht: Kluwer.

Signposts – vekhi. 1986. Trans. M. Shatz and J. Zimmermann. Irvine, CA: Schlacks.

Stam, Per. 1998. *Krapula: Henry Parland och romanprojekt 'Sönder.'* Uppsala: Uppsala University Press.

Stepun, Fiodor. 1961. *Das Antlitz Russlands und das Gesicht der Revolution.* München: Kösel.

Swoboda, P. 1995. "Windelband's Influence of S. L. Frank," *Studies in East European Thought* 47, pp. 259–90.

Tarasti, Eero (ed.). 1999. *The Finnish School of Semiotics,* "Introduction." Bloomington: Indiana University Press, pp. 11–13.

———. 1990. "Scenes in the Semiotic History of the Baltic Countries" in

K. Sarje (ed.) *SIKSI* 2: 12–18. Helsinki: Nordisk Kunstcentrum/Nordic Arts Center.

———. 2000. *Existential Semiotics*. Bloomington, IN: Indiana University Press.

Vietroff, J. 1912. "L'influence de la philosophie de H. Bergson" in *Mouvement socialiste,* janvier.

Voloshinov, V. N. 1972. *Marksizm i filosofiia iazyka* [Leningrad: 1930]. Paris, The Hague: Mouton.

———. 1973. *Marxism and the Philosophy of Language*. New York, London, Ann Arbor: Seminar Press.

Vossler, Karl. 1925. *Geist und Kultur in the Sprache*. Heidelberg: Winter.

Vvedenskii, Alexandr. 1915. *Psikhologiia bez vsakoi metafiziki*. Petrograd: Stasulevitch.

———. *Filosofskie ocherki*. 1924. Prague: Plamia.

Wach, Joachim. 1932. *Typen Religiöser Anthropologie: Eine vergleichende Lehre vom Menschen im religionsphilosophische Denken von Okzident und Orient*. Tübingen: Mohr.

Walzel, Oskar. 1973. *Das Wortkunstwerk*: Mittel seiner Erforschung. Darmstadt: Wissenschaftliche Buchgesellschaft.

West, James D. 1995. "Art as Cognition in Russian Neo-Kantianism," *Studies in East European Thought* 47/3–4, pp. 195–223.

———. 1991. "Kant, Kant, Kant: the Neo-Kantian Creative Consciousness in Andrei Bely's Petersburg," in P.I. Barta (ed.): *The European Foundations of Russian Modernism*. Lewiston: Edwin Mellen: pp. 87–135.

Wortis, J. *Soviet Psychiatry*. 1950. Baltimore: William & Wilkins.

Zhirmunskii, Viktor. 1970. "V. Sezemanni atminti" (Preface to Sesemann, *Estetika*), 3–6.

Index of Subjects: